Dzogchen

The Ultimate Guide to the Practice, Meditation, Teachings, and History of a Tradition in Tibetan Buddhism

© Copyright 2021

The contents of this book may not be reproduced, duplicated or transmitted without direct written permission from the author.

Under no circumstances will any legal responsibility or blame be held against the publisher for any reparation, damages, or monetary loss due to the information herein, either directly or indirectly.

Legal Notice:

This book is copyright protected. This is only for personal use. You cannot amend, distribute, sell, use, quote or paraphrase any part or the content within this book without the consent of the author.

Disclaimer Notice:

Please note the information contained within this document is for educational and entertainment purposes only. Every attempt has been made to provide accurate, up-to-date, and reliable complete information. No warranties of any kind are expressed or implied. Readers acknowledge that the author is not engaging in the rendering of legal, financial, medical, or professional advice. The content of this book has been derived from various sources. Please consult a licensed professional before attempting any techniques outlined in this book.

By reading this document, the reader agrees that under no circumstances is the author responsible for any losses, direct or indirect, which are incurred as a result of the use of the information contained within this document, including, but not limited to, errors, omissions, or inaccuracies.

Your Free Gift (only available for a limited time)

Thanks for getting this book! If you want to learn more about various spirituality topics, then join Mari Silva's community and get a free guided meditation MP3 for awakening your third eye. This guided meditation mp3 is designed to open and strengthen ones third eye so you can experience a higher state of consciousness. Simply visit the link below the image to get started.

https://spiritualityspot.com/meditation

Contents

INTRODUCTION 1
CHAPTER 1: UNDERSTANDING THE NINE YANAS 3
   THE FOUR NOBLE TRUTHS 4
   THE SIGNIFICANCE OF HUMAN LIFE 6
   THE NINE YANAS 7
   THE THREE OUTER VEHICLES LEADING FROM THE ORIGIN 8
   THE THREE INNER VEHICLES 12
   THE THREE SECRET VEHICLES OF POWERFUL TRANSFORMATIVE
   METHODS 15
CHAPTER 2: DZOGCHEN – THE PINNACLE OF WISDOM 19
   TRADITIONAL ACCOUNTS OF DZOGCHEN 20
   DUMBFOUNDEDNESS OR BEDAZZLEMENT AND RIGPA IN DZOGCHEN ... 22
CHAPTER 3: SUTRA, TANTRA AND DZOGCHEN 29
   SUTRA - THE RENUNCIATION APPROACH 30
   TANTRA - THE TRANSFORMATION APPROACH 32
   DZOGCHEN - THE SELF-LIBERATION APPROACH 34
   UNDERSTANDING THE SEEMINGLY CONFLICTING PATHS OF SUTRA,
   TANTRA, AND DZOGCHEN 37
CHAPTER 4: THE SEVENTEEN TANTRAS 38
   IMPORTANT PROPONENTS OF THE SEVENTEEN TANTRAS 39
   THE SEVENTEEN TANTRAS 40

  NECKLACE OF PRECIOUS PEARLS 41
  KISSING OR THE UNION OF THE SUN AND MOON 41
CHAPTER 5: SEMDE TEACHINGS 44
  THE EIGHTEEN TANTRAS OF SEMDE 46
  KULAYARĀJA TANTRA 47
  THE FOUR YOGAS OF SEMDE 48
  A DZOGCHEN PRAYER TO THE GURU 49
CHAPTER 6: LONGDE TEACHINGS 50
  WHAT IS EMPTINESS OR SHUNYATA? 51
  SAMANTABHADRA'S ROYAL TANTRA OF ALL-INCLUSIVE VASTNESS 52
  SKY MEDITATION 54
CHAPTER 7: MENNGAGDE TEACHINGS 58
  SEVEN MIND TRAINING 59
  APPLYING THE DZOGCHEN PRACTICE RIGHT THROUGH YOUR LIFE 66
  THE MEASURE OF MIND TRAINING 68
  THE COMMITMENTS OF MIND TRAINING 68
  THE PRECEPTS OF MIND TRAINING 69
CHAPTER 8: GETTING READY FOR DZOGCHEN 72
  TRAINING IN THE PRELIMINARIES 74
  IMPORTANCE OF SAMATHA AND VIPASSANA MEDITATION 75
  CONVENTIONAL TRUTH AND ABSOLUTE OR UNCONVENTIONAL TRUTH 76
  THE POWER OF OUR EGO 77
  FORGIVENESS AND LETTING GO 79
  ACCUMULATION OF MERIT 79
  NGONDRO TEACHINGS 82
CHAPTER 9: HOW TO AWAKEN YOUR RIGPA 84
  RECOGNIZING THE ALAYA OF HABITS 84
  THE METHOD OF MEDITATION 85
  MADHYAMAKA ANALYTICAL MEDITATION 86
  MARIGPA - THE OPPOSITE OF RIGPA 88
  THE EFFULGENT RIGPA 91
  THE ESSENCE RIGPA 92
CHAPTER 10: THE SEMDZIN PRACTICE 94

CHAPTER 11: THE TREKCHO PRACTICE 101
    UNDERSTANDING KADAG TREKCHO 102
    MEDITATION TO ACHIEVE TREKCHO 104

CHAPTER 12: THE TOGAL PATH 109
    THE TOGAL PATH FOR A BEGINNER 111
    A SIMPLE, POWERFUL PRAYER TO DZOGCHEN MASTERS 112

CONCLUSION 114

HERE'S ANOTHER BOOK BY MARI SILVA THAT YOU MIGHT LIKE 116

YOUR FREE GIFT (ONLY AVAILABLE FOR A LIMITED TIME) 117

REFERENCES 118

Introduction

Let us start this book by looking at the way we lead our lives. We work hard and earn money and fame, and success. We use the money we've made to lead a "good" life and often hope to pass on the legacy to our children, who can also lead a "good" life.

The hooks and temptations offered by such a life are so strong that we forget the profound, subtle, and actual nature of reality. We are caught up in living life in the usual, easy way. For example, your thoughts right now may be, "Today is a Saturday. The sun is shining, and I'm going to watch movies and eat ice cream." The weekend goes like this.

Then, Monday comes. You have a routine appointment with your doctor, and suddenly you are brought to the realization that a deadly disease afflicts you. Now, you are extremely sad. So, you are happy when you "feel" free and while eating ice cream, and you are devastated when you hear of "bad" news.

Human life oscillates between extremely afflictive emotions so much we don't get a breath of time to focus on the true nature of reality. Dzogchen helps overcome afflictions and suffering – and adds value to your life.

The Dzogchen system is one of the most advanced and oldest systems of meditation, reaching the subtlest and deepest levels of our mind. Dzogchen has been part of the Nyingma and Bon traditions of Tibetan Buddhism from ancient times. Later, it was also incorporated into numerous Kagyu schools.

Dzogchen is an ancient, prehistoric form of belief system. However, today, the meditation techniques of Dzogchen are used beyond religious and philosophical needs. The meditation techniques prescribed in the Dzogchen system are employed outside Buddhist systems and in various other contexts, including:
- To calm the mind - at the very basic level
- To attain the level perfect state of *shamatha* - a state of mind entirely still and settled - at an advanced level

While the elements mentioned above might sound confusing, they are not. Dzogchen practice does not require you to leave your home or your usual way of life to live the life of a hermit. No! Dzogchen teaches you not to "fall asleep subconsciously" while leading a normal life.

This book initiates the beginner into the Dzogchen by sharing all its fascinating elements in brief and enticing them into the wonderful world of Tibetan Buddhism. And yet, even people with a good depth of knowledge in the study and practice of Dzogchen will find it interesting, considering that all vital elements are covered in one book.

So, read on, and don't hesitate to get lost in the wondrous and enlightening world of Dzogchen practice.

Chapter 1: Understanding the Nine Yanas

Buddhism is one of the world's oldest religious-cum-philosophical belief systems, with foundations laid in ancient India by Gautama Buddha. Guatama was a royal prince who gave up a life of luxury and wealth in search of enlightenment. After the death of Gautama Buddha, his teachings spread all over the world, primarily through Tibet and China, giving rise to different forms of Buddhism. Dzogchen is usually associated with Nyingma, an ancient form of Tibetan Buddhism founded by Padmasambhava.

And yet, Dzogchen goes back many centuries before this and is not limited to Tibet or Buddhism. There have been 12 great Dzogchen masters in ancient times. Dzogchen is the abbreviated form of the Tibetan word, "Dzogpachenpo," made up of two root words, namely "Dzogpa," which means "the end" or "complete" and "chenpo" which means "great." Therefore, Dzogchen is popularly translated as "The Great Perfection" or "The Great Completeness" and refers to the primordial nature inherent in all of us.

According to Dzogchen, all of us already have a perfected state within us. This state, called Buddhahood, needs no more perfection because the perfect state already exists. Like the sky, this perfect state is uncreated but spontaneously accomplished. Dzogchen helps you reach this perfect state through the nine vehicles or "yanas." But before we move on to the nine yanas, let us try to explain a few important Buddhist principles and the meaning of Dzogchen.

The Four Noble Truths

Buddhism is primarily rooted in the Four Noble Truths. All forms of Buddhism, whether Hinayana (better and more kindly called Theravada), Mahayana, Vajrayana, Mahamudra, Dzogchen practice, are founded on tenets called the Four Nobles Truths. These were shown to the world by the historical Buddha, or Shakyamuni, as he is known in Tibetan Buddhism. Here is a brief explanation of each of the above forms of Buddhist teachings:

- Hinayana - is primarily based on morality and ethics
- Mahayana - is a practice of great compassion
- Vajrayana - is a practice that combines compassion and wisdom
- Dzogchen - is the ultimate Buddhist practice according to which it is possible to achieve awakening or enlightenment or liberation in your current lifetime

The four noble truths are briefly discussed below:

The First Truth is the identification and acceptance of suffering in the world. The existence of suffering is an unequivocal aspect of Buddhism. It exists, so we feel pain, agony, anger, frustration, and all the negative emotions humans feel.

The Second Truth identifies the roots of suffering, namely desire and ignorance. In Buddhism, desire is defined by hankering after material and sensual pleasures and the desire for immortality, all of which are insatiable wants. Suffering is experienced when these desires are not met. Ignorance, according to Buddhism, is the inability to see the world as it is.

When we don't build our capability for mental concentration to receive deep insights into the world's true nature, this is called ignorance and is known to cause suffering. Vices such as greed, anger, frustration, hatred, and envy are all rooted in ignorance, as defined above.

The Third Truth states it is possible to achieve a transcendent free state called Nirvana which will end suffering. Through Nirvana, suffering ends in this life and on this Earth, and from the cycle of birth, death, and rebirth. Nirvana is the state of spiritual enlightenment.

The Fourth Truth charts a path called the Noble Eightfold Path to end suffering, and it comprises of:

    1. Right Understanding

    2. Right Thought

    3. Right Speech

    4. Right Action

    5. Right Livelihood

    6. Right Effort

    7. Right Mindfulness

    8. Right Concentration

This Noble Eightfold Path is categorized under three themes, namely:

    1. Good moral conduct includes understanding, thought, and speech.

    2. Mental development and meditation include action, livelihood, and effort.

3. Insight or wisdom, which includes mindfulness and concentration.

The Significance of Human Life

According to Buddhism, we have taken on multiple births in the past and will continue to take on multiple births in the future too. We can take on any kind of birth. We could be born as hungry ghosts and spirits, fish, insects, other kinds of animals, jealous and/or benign gods and goddesses, and more. Being born as a human is a very special privilege.

According to Dzogchen principles, human life is precious because only <u>by</u> receiving rebirth as a human do we have a chance to achieve enlightenment and liberation through Nirvana. Every human is a sentient comprising five aggregates, including sensation, matter, mental formations, perceptions, and consciousness. Every sentient being is born with the ability to know the true nature of reality. Every individual is born with the Buddha-nature, which allows us to know and realize the true nature of reality and dispel darkness and ignorance.

Rebirth in any other life form does not offer this opportunity. Therefore, we should not take our lives for granted. Human life is like a temporary vacation from taking lower life forms. If we don't take care and live our lives correctly, we can easily slip back to the lower realms.

After all, death is a certainty, and the only thing we have control of in this life as humans is to ensure we live it in a way that prevents our return to the lower realms. And this can be done by taking refuge in the Dharma Jewel. At the deepest level, the Dharma Jewel refers to the Third and Fourth Noble Truths. Let us see how.

As already explained, the Third Noble Truth refers to the importance of building our mind's capability to understand the true nature of this world. In the language of Dzogchen, we call the "true nature" "*rigpa*" or "*pure awareness.*" We all have access to pure awareness, our mental continuum's subtlest and purest level.

When we access our "rigpa," then we become free from all suffering and the causes of suffering. The rigpa is full of only positive qualities. According to Dzogchen, we must strive to identify and recognize "the face of our rigpa" because nearly all of us are unaware of its presence. And because we are unaware of our rigpa's presence and power, we cannot use it to our advantage to end suffering.

Now, we move on to the Fourth Noble Truth, which tells us the path to realizing pure awareness. When we gain access to rigpa and eliminate suffering and its causes from our life, then we become free from the cycle of birth and death. After all, regardless of the realm of life, whether it is the higher human life or lower realms of animals, insects, and plants, it is still "samsara." It is the uncontrollable whirlpool of births and deaths from which we need to be freed.

Interestingly, the cycle is "uncontrollable" because it is under the powerful influence of emotions and karma. Karma includes our actions, experiences, thoughts, and everything else we do when we live life subconsciously and mindlessly. When we gain the strength to look at our karma and the suffering it causes, then we become afraid, and we strive to come out of this vicious cycle.

Fear, in this context, does not mean the destructive emotion that drives us to panic. Fear in Tibetan Buddhism clears our minds and shows us the true nature of suffering, then shows us the path to be free of it. And that is the direction of Dzogchen. It is the direction that will take us to "rigpa," or pure awareness, each of us is born with.

The Nine Yanas

Sakyamuni, the name commonly used in Tibetan Buddhism to refer to Gautama Buddha, left behind an infinite number of teachings by which people can enter the Dharma. This depends on each person's temperament, attitude, and spiritual faculties. All these teachings can be categorized under three types or vehicles. Each is further divided

into three successive vehicles, ultimately leading to "nine successive stages or yanas," including:
- The three outer vehicles leading from the origin
- The three inner vehicles, comparable to asceticism practiced by Vedic followers, also called the outer classes of tantra
- The three secret vehicles, or the inner classes of tantra, consisting of extremely powerful transformative methods

Let us start by learning the term "yana" or vehicle. Yana is the means of conveyance that carries us forward on our life paths and allows us to experience higher and greater qualities of enlightenment. Now, let's look at each of the three vehicles.

The Three Outer Vehicles Leading from the Origin

So, why are these three outer vehicles called "*leading from the origin?*" The answer is simple. These three outer vehicles lead us from the origin of suffering rooted in samsara (repeated cycles of births and deaths) into liberation. And these vehicles facilitate this path to liberation from suffering by helping us abandon all the actions (or kleshas) that cause suffering. The three outer vehicles include:
- The Sravaka Vehicle
- The Pratyekabuddha Vehicle
- The Bodhisattva Vehicle

Each vehicle has these characteristics:
- An entry point - or the starting point for a practitioner
- The view - the elements the practitioner focuses on and what they perceive.
- Meditation - the form of meditation the practitioner uses to achieve the results.
- The conduct - how the practitioner lives his or her life

- The results - the outcome for the practitioner if he or she abides by the chosen vehicle. There are eight levels of fruition as follows (each of the four has two more levels, namely the emerging and the established):
  - The stream-enterer
  - Once-returner
  - Non-returner
  - Arhat

The Sravaka Vehicle - Sravaka, in this context, translates to "listening and proclaiming." Therefore, Sravakas (the ones who employ the Sravaka vehicle) depend on masters to teach them how to liberate themselves from the samsara and then proclaim what they have learned to others.

Entry Point - The Sravaka vehicle is the starting point for those yearning to escape from the clutches of samsara by themselves. These people receive one of seven prescribed Sravaka vows, including male or female lay practitioners, novice nun or monk, probationary nun, fully-ordained nun or monk. Once the chosen vow is received, these Sravakas live their lives and practice moral restraint as ordained in the vows.

View - Sravakas focus on all phenomena, including their five aggregates (or senses), and realize they do not have a personal self. However, they don't realize that all phenomena in this cosmos do not have a true reality. So, although Sravakas can perceive an indivisible moment of consciousness multiple times through their focused view, they do not realize the absence of phenomenal identity.

Meditation - They practice Vipasyana and Samatha meditation techniques. Using samatha meditation, sravakas can eliminate obstacles even while learning to cultivate factors and elements conducive to achieving the samadhi state. Through Vipasyana meditation, they focus on the 16 aspects of the four noble truths.

Conduct - Sravakas lead a life that avoids the two extreme lifestyles of excessive denial of sensual pleasures and self-punishment and overindulgence in sensual pleasures by employing the 12 ascetic practices.

Results - Sravakas can achieve one of the eight levels of fruition, which means they can abandon the kleshas or actions of the three realms.

The Pratyekabuddha Vehicle - The Pratyekabuddhas are self-awakened practitioners. They have a deeper knowledge of wisdom than the Sravakas. They don't need masters to manifest their knowledge and awakening. They can do so based on their own wisdom.

Entry Point - Like the Sravakas, the Pratyekabuddhas also choose one of the seven vows and lead their life strictly according to these vows.

View - Pratyekabuddhas realize the absence of the personal self. However, realizing the absence of phenomenal identity is not partially achieved. They are yet to realize the truth behind the indivisible moments of consciousness, although they realize that the perceived objects are not real.

Meditation - Pratyekabuddhas focus on the 12 links of interdependent origination. These links arise in progressive order, and how they cease in the reverse order.

Conduct - Pratyekabuddhas, like the Sravakas, live by the 12 rules of ascetic practice.

Results - Pratyekabuddhas can attain the level of pratyekabuddha arhats. However, those with sharper faculties can achieve a rhinoceros-like level. In comparison, those with duller faculties tend to achieve a parrot-like level. The Pratyekabuddhas work with three specific prayers, including:
- They pray this will be their last birth without buddhas and sravakas

- They pray that they attain awakening on their own wisdom and without depending on any teacher
- They pray that they teach others silently and with only hand gestures.

The Bodhisattva Vehicle - Also called the vehicle of characteristics, the Bodhisattva path has all the characteristics needed to bring about the ultimate result, the Buddhahood.

Entry Point - Bodhisattvas live their life to benefit others. They are motivated by "bodhicitta," a life principle characterized by their wish to establish all sentient beings on the level of Buddhahood, the ultimate fruition. At the level of Buddhahood, there is freedom from suffering. Inspired in this way, Bodhisattvas take vows and live a life ordained and disciplined by these vows.

View - Bodhisattvas realize the complete absence of the personal self and the phenomenal identity through the "Mind-Only" approach. Bodhisattvas realize that all outer objects are nothing more than the projection of our inner mind, and they also claim that the all-encompassing consciousness is devoid of duality. They understand that all phenomena are a result of dependent origination, and in reality, are nothing but emptiness.

Meditation - They meditate to train their minds to realize the indivisibility of the two levels of reality. They also combine the samatha and vipassana meditation techniques to focus on the 37 factors of alignment sequentially.

Conduct - Bodhisattvas live according to the four means of attraction for the benefit of others and live by the six transcendent perfections for their own spiritual upliftment and benefit.

Result - Bodhisattvas attain Buddhahood, the ultimate fruit for any human.

The Three Inner Vehicles

Also called the three inner vehicles of Vedic-like asceticism, this category of yana consists of these three types:
- The vehicle of kriya tantra
- The vehicle of carya tantra
- The vehicle of yoga tantra

The Vehicle of Kriya Tantra - Kriya translates to "action," and therefore, the vehicle of action tantra is concerned primarily with external conduct and ritual cleanliness and purification practices.

Entry Point - The entry point for the vehicle of kriya tantra or mantra Vajrayana is ripening empowerment, of which there are two types. An empowerment is a ritual initiating a student into a particular tantric practice. This ritual represents an act of transmitting the power of the practice from the master to the student.

Water empowerment empowers the potential for ripening into the dharmakaya. Crown empowerment allows ripening into *rupakaya*. Once the vows for the ripening empowerment are taken, the initiate lives by and maintains the general samayas of the kriya yoga. Samayas are sets of precepts or vows which students have to adhere to after receiving empowerment.

View - The view as seen by this vehicle is that the nature of our mind is the wisdom of empty clarity. The mind sees things as existing or not existing, appearing or disappearing, or empty. The relative appearance is then focused on which need is to be purified until everything can be seen as the characteristics of the completely pure deity.

Meditation - Meditation is centered upon four realities, namely:
- The reality of oneself
- The reality of the deity
- The reality of mantra recitation
- The reality of concentration

Conduct - In this vehicle, the practitioner performs three types of ritual purification. These include changing three types of clothing, eating three types of white foods, and practicing mantra recitation along with ritual fasting.

Result - By walking on this path or vehicle, one can become a *Vidyadhara* (in the short-term) and a *Vajradhara* (in the long term). As a Vajradhara, one achieves the state of awakening on the same lines as one of the three Buddha families, namely:
- Vairochana - the family of enlightened body
- Amitabha - the family of enlightened speech
- Aksobhya - the family of enlightened mind

The Vehicle of Carya Tantra - Carya Tantra vehicle focuses on outward behavior, attitude, speech, and conduct as much as cultivating the practitioner's inner self. It is also called "*ubhaya* tantra," translating to "both the tantra" as it combines the characteristics of the kriya and yoga tantra.

Entry Point - The practitioner achieves maturity and wisdom through the means of five empowerments, including:
- Vajra empowerment
- Bell empowerment
- Name empowerment
- Water empowerment
- Crown empowerment

Following one of these empowerments, the practitioners maintain the samayas according to the particular texts relating to empowerment.

View - The practitioner sees everything and all phenomena of this cosmos as clear light. He realizes that everything is beyond conceptual comprehension. The relative is viewed as deities of the Vajradhatu.

Meditation - The practitioners view themselves as deity beings and focus on the wisdom deity who is regarded as a friend rather than as a divine being. They visualize the deity in front of them and then practice conceptual meditation on the form, syllable, and mudra of the deity and non-conceptual meditation on the absolute bodhicitta.

Conduct - Practitioners maintain the following conduct:
- Extremely unelaborate
- Unelaborate
- Elaborate

Results - In the short term, practitioners attain common accomplishments. In the long term, they achieve the ultimate goal of a vajradhara belonging to one of the four Buddha families. Three of them have been mentioned earlier, and the fourth family is that of the ratna family.

The Vehicle of the Yoga Tantra - This vehicle focuses on inner yogic meditation combining wisdom and skillful means.

Entry Point - The practitioner matures through the eleven empowerments, namely:
- The five empowerments of disciples, including water, bell, vajra, crown, and name
- The six empowerments of the master include irreversibility, seeing the secret reality, prophecy, authorization, praising encouragement, and confirmation

The practitioner maintains the samayas as prescribed in the particular texts related to each empowerment.

View and Meditation - The view and meditation are the same as for the Vehicle of Carya Tantra.

Conduct - Practitioners emphasize ritual purification and cleanliness. However, these are used merely as support.

Result - In the sense of worldly attainment, the practitioner achieves celestial vidyadhara. At the supermundane level, the practitioner attains ghanavyuha as one of the five Buddha families, which includes the four mentioned earlier. The fifth family is that of Amoghasiddhi, the family of enlightened activity.

The Three Secret Vehicles of Powerful Transformative Methods

These three are the inner classes of tantra and include:
- The vehicle of mahayoga
- The vehicle of anuyoga
- The vehicle of atiyoga

They are called "powerful transformative methods" because these vehicles contain powerful methods to transform all phenomena into a realm of purity and equality. Let us look at each of the three vehicles in a bit of detail:

The Vehicle of Mahayoga - This vehicle is called "maha" or great because it is not as simple as the ordinary yoga tantra. Through the Mahayoga tantra, a practitioner can see the magical display where emptiness and appearance are the same and inseparable.

Entry Point - The entry point for this vehicle is when the practitioner's mind is matured through receiving these empowerments:
- The ten outer benefitting empowerments
- The five inner enabling empowerments
- The three secret profound empowerments

With these empowerments, the practitioner maintains the prescribed samayas.

View - The practitioner views, establishes, and realizes the indivisibility of the two higher levels of reality through extraordinary ways of reasoning. The practitioner establishes and realizes that the seven riches of the absolute, which cause the appearance of essential nature, are spontaneously contained within pure awareness. The practitioner sees that all relative phenomena appear as "the mandala of the deities of the three seats."

Meditation - The practitioners of this vehicle of mahayoga use general stage yoga. They practice the three samadhis, including the purifying, perfecting, and ripening samadhis, ensuring the visualization is complete. After this, they seal and secure the life force with the instruction of the four nails. Through this meditation, practitioners can activate the vital points of the vajra body along with its essence, luminosity, and subtle energies.

Conduct - Practitioners maintain elaborate, unelaborate, and extremely unelaborate conduct.

Results - Initially, practitioners attain the four vidyadhara levels, all of which are part of the path to the ultimate fruition, which is the level of vajradhara unity.

The Vehicle of Anuyoga - This vehicle is called scriptural transmission anuyoga or "following yoga." The primary focus of this vehicle is to teach practitioners the path of following or passionately pursuing wisdom to reach the ultimate stage of knowing. The practitioner should also realize that all phenomena are manifestations of the indivisible unity of primordial wisdom and absolute space.

Entry Point - The entry point for the vehicle of anuyoga is when the practitioner's mind is matured through 36 empowerments with the four rivers. Namely when the outer, inner, accomplishing, and secret rivers are complete. The practitioner then maintains the samayas as prescribed in the texts.

View - Practitioners employ logical reasoning to determine and realize the ultimate truth, that all phenomena are manifestations of the three mandalas in their fundamental nature.

Meditation - There are two paths of meditation in this vehicle. The path of liberation uses two types of samadhi meditation, namely the non-conceptual and the conceptual samadhi. The non-conceptual samadhi is a state of resting that is aligned with the essence of the reality itself. The conceptual samadhi is that of deity practice where practitioners visualize the mandala of the supporting palace and supporting deities through the recitation of mantras. The path of skillful means calls for meditation practices of the upper and lower gateways to generate the wisdom of emptiness and bliss.

Conduct - The conduct of this vehicle goes beyond adopting or abandoning all phenomena knowing and realizing that all perceptions are nothing but manifestations of the wisdom of great bliss.

Results - When practitioners complete Anuyoga's five paths or five yogas, each of which has ten stages included in it, they reach the level of Samantabhadra.

The Vehicle of Atiyoga - Also called the "pith instruction atiyoga," this is the highest of all vehicles. Hence, the name "atiyoga" wherein "ati" translates to the "best" or "highest." This vehicle shows the path to realizing that all phenomena are mere appearances of the naturally-arising primordial wisdom, which by itself is beyond arising and ceasing.

Entry Point - When one's mind is matured through the "expressive power of awareness" empowerments, then the practitioner maintains the samayas of atiyoga as prescribed in the texts.

View - Practitioners focus on the three inseparable kayas of naturally-arising wisdom. The three kayas include:
- Dharmakaya - the empty essence of naked awareness lying beyond the ordinary mind.
- Sambhogakaya - the conscious nature of naked awareness.
- Nirmanakaya - the all-pervasive compassionate energy of naked awareness.

Meditation - The meditative approach of the atiyoga vehicle calls for breaking the resistance to primordial purity. There are two paths for this, one for the lazy and one for the diligent. The lazy can achieve liberation without effort through the direct realization of spontaneous presence. The diligent can achieve liberation through exertion.

Conduct - The conduct of atiyoga practitioners is free from hope, fear, adopting, and abandoning because everything is a manifestation of the reality itself.

Results - When practitioners perfect the four visions of the path, they achieve the level of supreme kaya and attain the level of glorious Samantabhadra, or the "unexcelled wisdom."

The nine yanas of Dzogchen combines and unites Buddha's teachings into a single path leading to enlightenment. The last of the vehicles (atiyoga) is Dzogchen underlines the transformative powers of Buddhism.

Chapter 2: Dzogchen — The Pinnacle of Wisdom

Dzogchen is an extremely advanced system of meditation at a deep and fundamental level of your mind. In this context, the mind refers to mental activity and cognitive engagement with objects that give rise to appearances.

As explained in the previous chapter, Dzogchen translates to "great completeness." The "completeness" refers to the concept that all Buddhahood qualities are complete at the rigpa (or pure or naked awareness). According to the 14th Dalai Lama, Dzogchen could be rooted in the Sanskrit word, "mahasandhi."

So, why is Dzogchen the perfect and the pinnacle of wisdom? According to the Dzogchen masters, it is the last and final vehicle or path to be followed after all the previous eight vehicles are mastered. Any student must necessarily treat the entire path as an interconnected entity. Each vehicle is to be learned and practiced with equal importance.

Traditional Accounts of Dzogchen

Historically, there are two traditional accounts of Dzogchen, namely the Nyingma and the Bon traditions. Let us look at each of these two in a bit of detail.

Nyingma Tradition - The Dzogchen teachings of Nyingma tradition originated in ancient Tibet and are attributed to 12 primordial "nirmanakaya" buddhas. "Nirmanakaya" buddhas are those who take physical form in time and space. Each of these 12 primordial buddhas appeared to different sets of people and disciples and revealed certain doctrines and teachings. The 12th Buddha in the Nyingma tradition is believed to be Buddha Shakyamuni, or the Enlightened One, who is revered as the founder of Buddhism.

Also, Buddha Samantabhadra (who, along with Buddha Shakyamuni and Bodhisattva Manjusri together form the Shakyamuni Triad in Mahayana Buddhism) passed on the Dzogchen teachings to Buddha Vajrasattva, a revered bodhisattva in Mahayana Buddhism. Buddha Vajrasattva then taught the Dzogchen practice to Garab Dorje, also known as Prahevraja, an Indian who is believed to be a semi-historic human. The details of his birth, life, and spiritual exploits are a combination of legend and history.

According to the Nyingma tradition, Garab Dorje learned the Dzogchen practice from Buddha Vajrasattva and then passed it on to Padmasambhava, who brought it to Tibet between the 8th and 9th centuries. Padmasambhava was helped by two other Indian masters, namely Vimalamitra and Vairochana.

In the 9th century, when the Tibetan Empire was destroyed, the scriptures containing the teachings of Padmasambhava (collectively referred to as "terma") were concealed. From the 10th century onward, the Nyingma tradition was revived in Tibet using the interpretations and teachings drawn from these concealed scriptures.

Bon Tradition - Another version, according to Bonpos, states that Dzogchen was established by the founder of the Bon tradition, Buddha Tonpa Shenrab Miwoche, who is believed to have lived around 18000 years ago. He was supposed to be the ruler of Tazik, a kingdom in the west of Tibet.

Is Dzogchen a Yana or Pure Wisdom?

The term Atiyoga and Dzogchen appeared in the Indian texts belonging to the 8th and 9th centuries. In these texts, Dzogchen practice is not called a separate Yana. Also, there is no record of any separate lineages or traditions under the name of Dzogchen outside Tibet. Therefore, it could be concluded that Dzogchen is unique to Tibet, influenced by multiple teachings from other traditions, including those from China and India.

Modern academics have two primary interpretations of the relationship between Buddhist tantric practices and Dzogchen:

- One interpretation is that Dzogchen is a distinct tradition different from Buddhist tantric systems, including the three inner and three secret vehicles defined in the Nine Yanas.
- Another interpretation is that Dzogchen is not different from the tantric Buddhist tradition and is drawn from there itself.

Whatever the interpretation, Dzogchen is considered perfect because it is a complete, exhaustive, and all-inclusive middle-way path to enlightenment. It avoids the two extremes of eternalism and nihilism. Dzogchen can be seen in two ways. The Dzogchen path classifies Tibetan Buddhism wisdom into inner, outer, and secret teachings through the Nine Yanas.

Another way to describe Dzogchen practice is by taking the ninth and last vehicle as the Dzogchen practice and everything else preceding it as being outside of Dzogchen practice. Yet, it encompasses all the wisdom of Tibetan Buddhism, considering the last and ninth vehicles can happen only when the previous eight are learned and mastered.

Dumbfoundedness or Bedazzlement and Rigpa in Dzogchen

According to Dzogchen, nothing must be added to rigpa or pure awareness, which is endless and beginningless. However, at lower levels, the functionalities of rigpa are not optimal. And the reason for the compromised functioning is the presence of bedazzlement or dumbfoundedness, which obscures the ultimate truth from the seeker. This bedazzlement arises along with rigpa, and like rigpa has no beginning or end, and has its own pure, threefold nature:

Primal Purity - The purity of dumbfoundedness or bedazzlement is primal and is completely devoid of all levels of cognition and awareness. Also, it is primarily pure of "all impossible ways of existing."

Spontaneously Establishing - Dumbfoundedness gives rise to all appearances and manifestations collectively referred to as "mental holograms."

Responsiveness - Dumbfoundedness emerges in response to the needs, causes, and conditions of others. It communicates and indulges passionately with these needs, causes, and conditions.

This three-fold pure nature of dumbfoundedness obscures rigpa's reflexive, pure awareness. It is also responsible for the faculties:

- The primal purity nature is responsible for the faculties of our mind
- The "spontaneously establishing" nature is responsible for the faculties of our body
- The "responsiveness" is responsible for our speech

When rigpa flows with dumbfoundedness, basis rigpa functions as an Alaya of habits. This term in the Dzogchen system represents limited awareness created by the mixing of basis rigpa (pure, naked awareness) with dumbfoundedness. This combination creates foundational awareness based upon which these elements are computed:

- Karmic potentials and tendencies
- Memories
- Disturbing emotions and attitudes
- Habits to learn, understand, and grasp impossible ways of existing

The primary and ultimate aim of Dzogchen meditation includes:

- The true cessation of dumbfoundedness and the consequent cessation of Alaya of habits
- The uninhibited and uncompromised functioning of the rigpa, including all its good qualities for the full benefit of all

As already explained earlier in this book, Dzogchen forms part of the Bon and Nyingma traditions of Tibetan Buddhism. In the Nyingma classification of Nine Vehicles or Yanas, Dzogchen is referred to as "Atiyoga," the highest and the best of the six inner and secret tantra vehicles.

Although Dzogchen meditation techniques are used to calm and settle a disturbed mind in the modern world, Dzogchen practice includes the extensive study and practice of the outer and inner preliminaries to attain liberation and enlightenment

The Outer Preliminaries - The outer preliminaries of the Dzogchen system include these six elements:

- **The precious human life** - Human life is precious because liberation from samsara is possible only through human life. It is imperative to ensure we do not slip back into lower life realms.
- **Impermanence** - All phenomena are impermanent, and every moment changes under the influence of various causes and conditions.

- **The sufferings of samsara** - Samsara is the uncontrollable, recurring rebirth caused by karma, disturbing emotions, and attitudes.
- Karmic cause and effects
- **Liberation from samsara through renunciation** - This refers to a definite decision to be liberated from the sufferings of samsara. It is based on the conviction that complete cessation of suffering is possible, provided one is truly willing to sacrifice desires, the true causes of suffering.
- A healthy and strong relationship with a qualified spiritual teacher - Four levels of teachers are defined in Buddhism, namely:
- Buddhism professor
- An instructor of Dharma
- A ritual and meditation trainer
- A spiritual mentor

In the Nyingma system, the study and practice of the outer preliminaries are a prerequisite to the study and practice of the six inner preliminaries.

The Inner Preliminaries - The inner preliminaries include the study and practice of the following elements:
- **Refuge or safe direction along with prostration** - A safe direction is a life path that one follows to be protected from true suffering.
- **Love- and compassion-based bodhicitta** - Love is one's wish for others' happiness and working for the welfare of others even at the cost of self-sacrifice. Compassion is the wish for others to be free of suffering, similar to the wish to free oneself of suffering and its true causes.
- **Vajrasattva purification** - Vajrasattva is a Buddha figure that represents the purity of the mind.

- **Mandala offering** – Something offered or presented to benefit and bring happiness to someone else.
- **Chod offering of the practitioner's body** - Chod is an advanced tantra practice designed to cut off attachment to one's body.
- **Guru yoga** – This is another advanced tantric practice. Here, one visualizes one's qualities of body, mind, and speech joining with the good qualities of the teacher to provide spiritual uplifting.

After completing the six outer and inner preliminaries, tantric empowerment or initiation must be received following by strictly maintaining the vows taken by the practitioners. To practice the ultimate Dzogchen or Atiyoga (which is the final and the last and the transformative methods of the three secret vehicles), practitioners need to master the first two as well, namely:

- **Mahayoga tantra practice** - the first of the three secret vehicles in which the practitioner works with deity figures of Buddha along with mantras.
- **Anuyoga tantra practice** - the second of the three secret vehicles in which the practitioner works with subtler elements such as energy drops, channels, and subtle winds.

The practice of Dzogchen is too subtle and difficult for individual success unless you have prepared yourself well. This can be done through deep awareness and building a strong positive force (or merit) using the above practices. Additionally, the guidance of a qualified inspirational master is essential.

At a very basic level, Dzogchen meditation begins with silencing our mental activity to our thoughts of this and that. Each thought and moment of mental activity rises up, recedes, and ceases. Dzogchen practitioners can easily identify this process if they have studied and practiced the Madhyamaka presentation on emptiness or voidness.

The Madhyamaka is a Mahayana school of Indian Buddhism in which there is no assertion of any established existence. All traditions of Tibetan Buddhism study and practice the Madhyamaka along with three other Indian Buddhism schools. According to Madhyamaka, voidness or emptiness is defined as a complete absence of an identifiable "me" controlling or observing thought processes.

Being mindful of the arising, receding, and ceasing of each moment and each thought, verbal, conceptual thought liberates itself automatically. This means it disappears on its own, and it is then possible to identify and settle into a state between two thoughts.

The next state of Dzogchen meditation focuses on the simultaneous arising, receding, and ceasing of thoughts at each microsecond level, an even smaller unit of time than a moment. Achieving the ability to distinguish thoughts in microseconds is exceedingly difficult. At this level, one perceives the sensory information of only one sense. For example, only the color of a shape or object. This one-sensory microsecond happens before the information from the other senses is synthesized for the brain to create a mental synthesis, labeling it as "this" or "that" object.

Once this practice is perfected, the next level would be to focus on the space between the microseconds. At this level, we can access the Alaya of habits. Even at this level, it is limited awareness only because the rigpa is still mixed with dumbfoundedness.

Dzogchen meditation calls for you to go deeper into your mind and thoughts to identify and experience the cognitive spaces between subtler time and space limits. This is until you can distinguish the threefold nature of deep awareness, namely its primal purity, spontaneous establishing, and responsiveness.

To achieve this level, practitioners need special methods and the help of a Dzogchen master to break down and understand our minds at deeply subtle layers of time and space. This is only possible when the practitioner has oiled and greased the energy channels by previous levels of anuyoga, wherein all gross levels of mental activity cease on their own with no conscious effort.

When dumbfoundedness ceases, our Alaya of habits becomes effulgent rigpa, which is also called "appearance-making basis rigpa." This form of rigpa actively gives rise to cognitive appearances but also actively cognizes them. At the level of effulgent rigpa, the rising of cognitive appearances or mental holograms is more prominent than cognizing them.

However, Dzogchen practitioners need to delve deeper. Focusing on the rising, receding, and ceasing of microseconds of appearances in effulgent rigpa, the practitioner learns to identify and recognize the essence rigpa. Essence rigpa is pure awareness and is that "cognitive sphere" or "open space" within which effulgent rigpa operates. At this level, mental holograms do arise. The practitioner can cognize them, with the cognition ability being more prominent than the arising of mental appearances.

When one remains focused and stays at this level of rigpa, the individual attains a "breakthrough" wherein a "path of seeing" appears, which is the third of the five pathway minds that leads to enlightenment. The "path of seeing" is the level of mind achieved by arya sharvakas, arya pratyekabuddhas, and arya bodhisattvas. At this level of mind, they can eliminate doctrinal obscurations.

The practice of Mahayoga tantra using Buddha figures paves the way for effulgent rigpa to give rise to and identify itself as a rainbow body, a "light body" as against the body made of ordinary aggregates. In this rainbow body, the gross, ordinary aggregates dissolve, similar to how a rainbow dissolves when the light-water connection is broken.

This experience is the cause for attaining the Form Bodies of a Buddha, a stage described in Dzogchen as the "leap-ahead stage," equivalent to an "accustoming pathway mind," a state of mind achieved by arya sharvakas, arya pratyekabuddhas, and arya bodhisattvas.

Enlightenment is achieved when effulgent and essence rigpa both become equally prominent. Moreover, driven by the compassionate and loving nature maintained by the practitioner right through the Dzogchen practice, they benefit all beings to the fullest possible extent.

While Dzogchen appears to be a direct path of settling into our mind's natural state, it is possible to realize pure rigpa by recognizing our cognitive experiences. The process itself is not at all easy. There is a tremendous amount of effort needed to achieve the state of Dzogchen. It is impossible until the practitioner has learned, lived, and practiced right through their previous lives the earlier stages of the path to enlightenment and freedom of suffering.

It would be naive and foolish to think it is possible to practice and live by the tenets of the Dzogchen principle easily and with little effort. Or even without the guidance of an experienced Buddhist monk or guru. Yet, it is possible to use the elements, ideas, and thoughts given in this book to think about the Dzogchen practice and see how you can begin the journey at the correct starting point. This book is the perfect place to get your preparations in place before you identify and find your spiritual master to move on in the journey.

Chapter 3: Sutra, Tantra and Dzogchen

Theoretically, in the Nyingma tradition across all lineages, masters teach all the yanas and the connected sutras, tantra, and Dzogchen, along with the subdivisions. But, practically, most teachers focus only on one particular yana, mostly that one that is aligned with their own teaching methods and beliefs.

One of the most important aspects of Buddhism is that it is not a "uniform" religion. It is not something that can be referred to as "one-size-fits-all." Buddhism is one of those few religions wherein there are so many different paths to reach Buddhahood. Each of us has the freedom to choose one that "best fits" our capabilities and personalities.

Therefore, it is important to know the advantages and disadvantages of each yana to choose what is best for you. Each of the nine yanas has a base, path, and outcome or result. As is clear from the names, the base is where you are, and the result is where the yana can take you.

The path of every vehicle has its own texture, flavor, and style. Interestingly, practitioners do not spend as much time and energy on the base or the result as they do on the path. If the path does not suit you, then you will not be motivated to walk the path to reach the result.

Buddhism prescribes three approaches to freeing yourself from suffering and the cycle of samsara. These three approaches include renunciation, transformation, and self-liberation. Each of these three corresponds to three yanas or vehicles, namely Sutra, Tantra, and Dzogchen. Renunciation is Sutra's path, tantra's path is transformation, and Dzogchen's path is self-liberation.

Sutra - The Renunciation Approach

Renunciation is a common approach in Buddhism. When the transformative powers of the Tantra path and the self-liberating approach of the Dzogchen path are not feasible or effective for certain practitioners, they choose the path of renunciation. Here, they keep away and renounce situations that provoke negativity and negative consequences.

As practitioners delve deeper into this practice, they can renounce emotions and the ideas connected to any situation. They are thus freeing themselves from the negative consequences of their reactions and responses to these situations. The renunciates cultivate compassion for others when they achieve peace of mind.

Monasticism and monastic life is the best environment to practice renunciation. One withdraws from the world, including social and family ties, gives up all possessions, including their desires and needs, and enters a monastery to live the life of a monk or nun. Celibacy and abstinence from alcohol are key elements in helping renunciates from getting stirred up by their desires. In fact, as a way of not being tempted, people who choose this approach are often taught to see the world as unclean, corrupt, and repulsive. Some even go to the extent of treating the human body as something that deserves only revulsion and subjugation.

The human ego is viewed as a poisonous tree whose roots have to be removed and killed one by one. The practitioner's every conduct and habit must be examined to remove and eliminate anything against the grain of renunciation. To achieve this, multiple levels of rules and conduct are available, which have to be strictly followed and adhered to by practitioners.

Sutra is the term that describes the scriptures of the yana. However, Sutra is also used as a short form of "Sutrayana," a term that usually means "all non-tantric Buddhism." So, Sutrayana can be defined as the vehicle (or yana) based on the sutras (or scriptures). In the Pali language, sutras are called "suttas." At this point, it might make sense to know that the scriptures of Tantra Buddhism are called "tantras" and not "sutras."

The foundation or base of Sutra (or Sutrayana) is to recognize and accept that our understanding of worldly satisfaction is not correct. The path of Sutrayana is renunciation which means a practitioner withdraws from the world to free themselves from its pleasures and pains. This withdrawal from the world keeps their emotions balanced and at peace.

As can be seen, this path is not aligned with having a family, being in a profession, etc. This is why monasteries were built and continue to be inhabited by people who choose the path of the Sutra. So, while Sutra is effective for those willing to give up worldly life entirely, it is not suitable for those unwilling to do so. The final point of the Sutra is to recognize emptiness.

Renunciation is a widely taught and popular concept practiced in the western world. However, students do not have to abandon their families, professions, and materialistic lives to live in a monastery. Instead, the Sutra practices are aimed to calm the mind by abstaining from the intensity of emotions and circumstances and situations presented by life.

Tantra - The Transformation Approach

Human emotions are almost always in conflict with our free experience. Emotions like anger, irritation, anxiety, compulsiveness, depression, etc., continually affect our efforts to correct our situations and experiences. These emotions hinder accepting reality as it is.

The transformational approach in Tibetan Buddhism is designed to manage these emotions effectively. This approach does not teach you to eliminate emotions but to celebrate them and include them in your life experiences without taking them very seriously.

The transformational approach helps you understand that emotions mean something to us and the world around us. That is why these emotions control us and drive us to react and/or respond in certain ways. If you can delink the connection between emotions and your responses to them, it is possible to embrace emotions without giving them control over you and your life.

For example, if you are angry at someone, then the emotional perception is anger. This automatically drives you to show angry behavior. Here are some easily relatable and common responses to emotions like anger:

- I don't like you because you said something I don't like.
- I am angry at what you did and will hurt you to get revenge.

Even if we don't actually say these words to people who have hurt or angered us, we are so hardwired to these responses we unconsciously think of them. Consequently, we feel driven to act on these responses too. With the transformational approach, it is possible to disconnect the emotion from the response it triggers.

When you disconnect the two, emotions become a source of energy that can be channelized to better use. With this disconnection, you can experience the emotions in their entirety without judging, suppressing, or analyzing them. As you learn and practice transforming your emotions, you learn to look at all circumstances without judging them and appreciate them. Emotions arise in your mind without the accompanying boredom, compulsiveness, or resentment.

When you enjoy the energy of the emotions without the accompanying burdens, the impetus to connect events and circumstances to conflicted feelings is released. Ultimately, the impetus to connect with conflicted actions also gets released.

The base of tantra is the recognition and realization of emptiness which results from sutra. And to achieve this requires dedicated meditation practice for several years. The path of tantra is very complex and layered. It calls for the learning and mastery of highly complicated and difficult doctrines and rituals. While tantra may not really be suitable for novices and beginners.

And yet, if one feels inspired by the brilliant, magical, colorful, poetic, emotional, and dynamic path of tantra, then you could be ready for Tantric ngondro. Tantric ngondro is a set of practices that leads you to the base of yana. Tantric ngondro has the same result as sutra, which is the realization of emptiness. But the path feels like tantra and not Sutra. Tantra can be an excellent vehicle to choose from in these circumstances:

- A good level of confidence in yourself and your life path
- When you are motivated by altruism
- If you are open to experimenting with unknown and unfamiliar situations and experiences

A word of caution here might make sense. Practicing Tantra rituals could involve the deliberate provoking of negative emotions. This can be very dangerous if not done in the right environment and under the strict supervision of qualified masters. Therefore, tantra has the dubious distinction of being attractive to some and totally unattractive to others. The result of tantra is freedom from feeling trapped by convention and indoctrination, from conflicting emotions, and from constricted expectations.

Dzogchen - The Self-Liberation Approach

Self-liberation is all about allowing all forms of energy, especially emotional energy, to remain and be as it is. Often, we are driven to interfering with our emotional energy. For example, even when we are on vacation, temporarily free from the stresses of routine life. Instead of being happy with our situation, we wish for many things such as:

- We wish the wine options were better
- We wish we could have gone to a better place
- We wish we had a better figure so we look as good as someone else

One of the biggest interfering thoughts that often mar our vacation is that the period of peace and calm will soon end, and we would have to get back to the rush and mess of a stressful life. We become "project managers" of our own lives, trying to allow our likes to come into our lives while keeping out our dislikes.

All these interfering thoughts drive us to "take action" and "manipulate" our lives, hoping that unpleasantness and suffering will disappear automatically into blissful oblivion. This is really not what happens! The concept of self-liberation is to let go of this need to "manipulate" and "take action." When we take this approach, we are free to experience and engage with life experiences directly and uncompromisingly.

When we allow our lives and the accompanying experiences and emotions as they are, we free ourselves from the burden of habits and preconditioned and preordained likes and dislikes. Consequently, we are free from the negative effects of conservative anxieties and routine personal expectations.

We are also free from the idea of what we should be and what we should not be, or what we must do and we must not, or worrying about the future and regretting the path, and so forth. All the energy typically used up for these unproductive ideas, actions, and thoughts can now be channeled into experiencing and engaging with every moment of our lives in a profound and meaningful way.

This energy-filled state of mind clears our heads and brings distinct clarity into our thoughts. Also, we are free to use this freed-up energy to enhance creativity, vitality, and generosity in our lives. All these elements are useful in benefiting yourself and the people around you, and this idea is the pith of Buddhist enlightenment.

Many people are attracted to Dzogchen because it is believed to be "the highest and perfect teaching of Buddhism." Contrarily, Buddhism itself emphasizes the importance of choosing the most useful path to you right now. As already explained, the base of Dzogchen is rigpa, or pure, naked awareness, or temporary enlightenment. Dzogchen practice aims to identify and grasp the spaces between momentary thoughts and, at a deeper level, the space between microseconds.

You can easily understand this "rigpa" is quite elusive, and grasping it is much easier said than done. Very few people are qualified to practice, and even fewer are qualified to be masters of Dzogchen. As a novice, Dzogchen looks like it is out of your reach. In such a circumstance, what is the use of learning about Dzogchen?

Yes, it is very useful because the Dzogchen ngondro can take you to the base of Dzogchen, which is rigpa. To do this, the only prerequisite from a novice is the willingness to learn and practice. Therefore, if Dzogchen practice is a good fit for your personality and need, it is a great place to start your journey with Tibetan Buddhism.

Dzogchen practices and teachings are powerful, clear, elegant, and simple too. In fact, the worldview expressed in Dzogchen is so simple and commonsensical that the rather esoteric and layered teachings can be easily misunderstood as being plain common sense.

You need only to drop all conventional preconceptions about yourself and your life and allow the experience to "be as it is." This approach is possible for anyone and everyone, at least theoretically. It takes a lot of patience and dedication to put the concept into practice. But this too is possible, providing you are willing to learn and be patient with yourself and your mind.

The practicality and logic in Dzogchen are highly popular and aligned with the thinking process of scientists, businessmen, and engineers. The flip side is that Dzogchen is quite dry and abstract, and learning from a master is a must, especially after a certain point of self-learning. So, starting with Dzogchen ngondro is a great way to build depth in your learning and mastering Dzogchen.

Another interesting aspect of Dzogchen is that the base, path, and result are the same, namely liberation. Sutra is often referred to as the "slow vehicle." Tantra is called the "fast vehicle," and Dzogchen is called the "instantaneous vehicle." The reason for this reference is that Dzogchen really does not have a process. It is simply being liberated.

This sense of liberation can be achieved through meditation which teaches us to believe in and trust the true nature of reality. And when this trust is achieved, we automatically abandon our need and desire to control anything.

Understanding the Seemingly Conflicting Paths of Sutra, Tantra, and Dzogchen

The seemingly different paths of the three vehicles could lead to conflicts, and sometimes, even animosity between students of different schools. It is, therefore, important to remember that the apparent contradictions in the three paths are only due to the different approaches taken by the three vehicles.

In reality, there is no conflict because none of the approaches is the "ultimate truth." They are all merely paths to reach the "ultimate truth," which remains unchanged regardless of the vehicle you choose to use. Some tips might help you choose the path that is most suitable for your personality:

- If the method used by the potential teacher and path is based on withdrawing from the stimuli of problems and causes of suffering, this method is useful for those practicing Sutra.
- If it is to help you accept and embrace emotions vividly and without resisting them, it is suitable for tantra.
- If the method is to help you simply experience life without trying to change anything in it, then it is the path of Dzogchen.

Chapter 4: The Seventeen Tantras

The seventeen tantras of the esoteric instruction cycle are viewed as terma or treasure in Tibetan Buddhism, specifically in the Dzogchen tradition. Terma is a word used in Tibetan Buddhism to describe a valuable object hidden under the earth, in a rock or crystal, in a lake, medicinal or magical herb, or any other secret space. These secrets are hidden for future discovery at appropriate times by capable masters.

The seventeen tantras, which have various other names within the Dzogchen discourse, including Nyingtik, Upadesha, or Menngagde, are considered terma. This is because they have been hidden by Dzogchen masters to be used at appropriate times in the future. While each of these seventeen tantras is sufficient by itself, they are also interconnected and interrelated because they are rooted in the one common practice of Dzogchen.

Important Proponents of the Seventeen Tantras

The seventeen tantras are also viewed in terma tradition. They are considered hidden in the "mind of a guru" to be imparted to students prepared and ready to accept the teachings. The seventeen tantras are associated with sacred texts and literature believed to be passed on to Garab Dorje, a quasi-historical individual around the 5th century. The teachings were then passed on to future lineages through various important Dzogchen masters and teachers, including:

Manjusrimitra - This Indian Buddhist scholar was the most important student of Garab Dorje. He is believed to have been born in a village close to Bodh Gaya and was a highly revered and respected student of Nalanda University. Most of his works are contained in a tantric collection titled Mañjuśrīnāmasamgīti.

Shri Singha - Shri (sometimes spelled as Sri) Singha was the dharma-son of Manjusrimitra. It is believed that he took the Atiyoga lineage to Andhra, a key federal state in South India.

Padmasambhava - This 8th-century Indian Buddhist scholar and master is referred to as Guru Rinpoche. Many legendary stories are woven around this master, and Tibetan Buddhists revere him as the "second Buddha." The Nyingma tradition was founded by Padmasambhava.

Jnanasutra - He was believed to be the spiritual brother of Vimalamitra and his teacher too. He was one of the earliest practitioners of Dzogchen.

Vimalamitra - He was an 8th-century Indian Buddhist monk and a student of Sri Singha and Jnanasutra. He is believed to have taken a vow to be reborn every 100 years. Some famous Dzogchen masters believed to be Vimalamitra's incarnation include Rigzin Jigme Lingpa, Khenchen Ngagchung, and Kyabje Drubwang Penor Rinpoche.

Avalokiteshvara - He is considered to be the earthly incarnation of Buddha Amitabha, the self-born eternal Buddha. He is believed to have been the guardian of humankind in the interval between the death of the historical Buddha and the birth of the future Buddha, Maitreya.

The Seventeen Tantras

It is believed that Sri Singha divided the Pith Instruction of Buddhism into four sub-sections, namely:
- The Exoteric Cycle
- The Esoteric Cycle
- The Secret Cycle
- The Supreme Secret Cycle

The seventeen tantras are part of the text collectively known as the "Supreme Secret Cycle," which was the last of the four most sacred tantras in the Nyingma Dzogchen tradition. Let us look at each of the seventeen tantras in a bit of detail.

Self-Liberated Awareness - The Sanskrit name for this tantra is *"mahā vidyā svamukti sarva ghaṭṭita tantra,"* the keyword being "svamukti" which translates to "self-liberation" in Sanskrit.

The Mirror of the Heart of Vajrasattva - The Sanskrit name is *"vajrasattva cittādarśa tantra."* This text forms part of the supporting text of Vimalamitra's work on Dzogchen titled "Nyingtik." The Mirror of the Heart of Vajrasattva tantra teaches that lamps are the self-display of awareness. This text lists 21 different instructions suitable for people with different proclivities and propensities along with the practice of instructions.

The Mirror of the Mind of Samantabhadra - Referred to as *"samantabhadra cittādarśa tantra,"* in Sanskrit, this text is an important document for Dzogchen practitioners.

Necklace of Precious Pearls

Lion's Perfect Expressive Power - In Sanskrit, this tantra is called *"mahā siṃha parākrama pūrṇṇa tantra."*

Shining Relics of Enlightened Body - Called *"śrī gagana śarīra jvala mahā tantra"* in Sanskrit, this tantra is also related to Buddhist relics.

Kissing or the Union of the Sun and Moon

Blazing Lamp Tantra - The Sanskrit name is *"svarṇṇa puṣpa kānti ratnāloka jvala tantra."*

Direct Introduction Tantra - Referred to as "darśanopadeśa ratnācita kṣetra dhātu śāsana tantra" in Sanskrit, this text is a direct introduction to Dzogchen teachings.

Great Auspicious Beauty Tantra - In Sanskrit, this tantra is called "mahā svaccha suvarṇāpramāṇa śrī tantra." It teaches practitioners how to identify and establish awareness by knowing the true foundation of confusion and how to discern it from unmistaken wisdom.

Six Spaces or the Sixfold Expanse of Samantabhadra Tantra - The Sanskrit name is *"samantabhadrā vartta ṣaṣṭha tantra."*

Without Letters Tantra - The Sanskrit name of this tantra is *"anakṣara mahā tantra nāma ratna dhvaja rāja saṃtati dṛṣṭi gagana sama mahā tantra."*

Inlaid with Jewels Tantra - In Sanskrit, this tantra is titled *"sarva bhrānti pṛ kara ratna dhūrta mata tantra."*

A Mound of Jewels Tantra - The Sanskrit name of this tantra is *"ratna kūṭa mahā guṇoddeśa tantra rāja."*

Here is a take on some of these seventeen tantras to give you a glimpse into what they hold for you, should you choose to become a Dzogchen practitioner.

Self-existing Perfection - The Sanskrit name of this tantra is *"kāyālokoddiṣṭābhisiñca mahā svayambhū tantra."* This tantra teaches practitioners how to prepare themselves to become suitable receivers of the teachings by using four empowerments, namely:
- Water empowerment - Vase
- Secret empowerment
- Knowledge-wisdom empowerment
- Word or suchness empowerment

Consequence of Sound - The Sanskrit name of the Consequence of Sound tantra is *"ratnākara śabda mahā prasaṅga tantra."* It is believed to be the root of the seventeen tantras. Like that used in the Sanskrit title of this tantra, sound denotes the uncreated, unconditioned, immutable, and primordial sound of the cosmos also called "nada." This concept of the primordial, uncreated sound of the nada is where Buddhism and the ancient Vedic religion align.

The esoteric and exoteric motifs of speech and sound during the evocation of various permutations of mantras are ubiquitous elements in Buddhism. The uncreated, unmade sound of nada is seen as a metaphor for spiritual energy and a metaphor for the luminosity of the Five Pure Lights, essential Dzogchen teaching.

For the deluded, matter, which combines classical elements (or "mahabhuta"), including earth, fire, water, air, and space, seems to appear because of the non-recognition of the Five Pure Lights. Knowledge (or rigpa) is the absence of this delusion, and this level of knowledge is called "rainbow body." The Five Pure Lights are the Five Wisdoms which include:

The wisdom of suchness is also called Dharmadhatu or the awareness of "sunyata" or nothingness. It is the universal basis for the other four wisdoms.

The wisdom of mirror-like awareness is the awareness of the absence of duality of thought and content. These are always united, just as the mirror and its reflections are always one and the same.

Self-Arising Awareness - The sanskrit term for this tantra is *"sarva tathāgata samādhi paribhāṣā jñāna samudāya sūtra mahāyāna guhyānuttara tantra sarva dharmākara sarva buddhānyaśayam mantraikajnāna mahāsandhyarthaprakatatantra vidyāsvodayamahātantranāma."* The Tibetan name is "Rigpa Rangsar." This tantra teaches view, conduct, and meditation, the common and most basic spiritual elements found in Nyingma tradition, in particular, and in Tibetan Buddhism, in general.

Necklace of Precious Pearls - The Sanskrit name of this tantra is *"ratna muṣṭi mūlā tantra."* When Buddhist spiritual masters are cremated, it is believed that their ashes contain crystal - and pearl-shaped objects - which become "Buddhist relics." The general term for this is "Sarira." These relics are believed to invoke and spread grace and blessings to the people associated with them.

Kissing or the Union of the Sun and Moon - The Sanskrit name is *"mahā sūrya candra ghana guhya tantra."* This tantra describes an individual's experience during "bardo," an intermediate state between life and death after the person passes away. This tantra explains how a person can follow his master's instructions during the intermediate state to receive enlightenment and choose to be reborn in the realm of nirmanakaya. In this realm, the individual achieves Buddhahood, thereby being free of samsara and rebirths.

Chapter 5: Semde Teachings

Here is a brief summary of what you have learned about Dzogchen until now. Although Dzogchen is associated with the Nyingma tradition of Tibetan Buddhism, the concept itself is extremely ancient. Dzogchen practice is all about finding the "primordial state of rigpa or pure awareness."

Dzogchen also refers to the "highest perfection" state in the Vajrayana practice, which practitioners achieve through mantra recitation and visualization of the deity. There are three series or lineages of Dzogchen teachings, namely:

- The Mind Series (Semde) - This series is about resting one's mind in dharmadata
- The Space Series (Longde) - Resting effortlessly. Also called transmission lineage
- The Secret Instruction Series (Menngagde) - Resting without accepting or rejecting. This lineage is also known as the oral lineage

It is important to remember that the three series do not represent three different schools conflicting with one another. Instead, they are merely three different approaches to the same goal: to achieve the natural, basic, primordial state.

Also, a common concept in Buddhist teachings is taking various approaches to suit the faculties and capabilities of different practitioners. These three series are often seen as appropriate for low-level, middle-level, and high-level faculties, respectively.

This chapter is dedicated to Semde or the Mind Series. This is attributed to the lineages of Sri Singha and Vairotsana. Semde emphasizes the totality of phenomena believed to be nothing more than the projections and apparitions of our minds.

Semde focuses on the nature of the mind and contemplation. It defines contemplation as the process by which practitioners look thoughtfully at something for a long time to achieve an inner vision and to transcend the intellect. Often prayers or meditation methods are used for this. Contemplating in this way helps to achieve a content-free mind which is then directed toward awareness of divinity.

The primary method of meditation used in Semde is called Zhine (also called object meditation), where the practitioners use a single object to meditate on. At first, the object is a visual, tangible one. Later on, the object evolves into an empty space. The primary emphasis of the Mind Series is on the primordial purity called "Kadag" or "Tregcho," which calls for the complete relaxation of the body, speech, and mind.

Dzogchen refers to the eyes as the gates of wisdom. When "*trekcho,*" the complete relaxation, is achieved, then the light chains or vajra chains just remain still waiting for your perception. To see the vajra chains, you must first develop a sense of "carelessness," which helps stop the light chains.

This sense of "carelessness" is about taking a non-caring attitude which helps to slow down the light chains, an essential step to cutting through and slowing down the light chains. The more the light chains are cut through, the more they appear. These light chains are connected to the speed of the brain and the physical body. It is possible to see your own brain when you have been able to cut through and slow down the light chains sufficiently using this practice.

In Semde teachings, there are no oral teachings or symbolic gestures. There is only mind-to-mind transmission. Usually, the student should be excellently prepared for receiving teachings. Even the master should have a very high level of wisdom, knowledge, and compassion. Only in such a situation can the transmission succeed. For example, the teachings transmitted by the primordial Buddha Samantabhadra gave to Vajrasattva through the mind alone.

In the Mind Lineage teachings, there is almost the complete absence of duality. It is as if there is no separation between the teacher and the student, and both are amid one awareness.

The Eighteen Tantras of Semde

The Semde describes its teachings through eighteen tantras and four yogas. The eighteen tantra texts of Semde include:

The Great Potency - The Tibetan name is *"rtsal chen sprug pa."*

The Cuckoo of Presence - The Tibetan name is *"rig pa'i khu byug."*

Great Garuda in Flight - The Tibetan name is *"khyung chen lding ba."*

Refining Gold from Ore - The Tibetan name is *"rdo la gser zhun."*

Great Space Never Waning Banner Scripture - The Tibetan name is *"mi nub rgyal mtshan nam mkha' che."*

Spontaneous Summit Scripture - The Tibetan name is *"rtse mo byung rgyal."*

King of Space - The Tibetan name is *"rnam mkha'i rgyal po."*

Jewel-Encrusted Bliss Ornament - The Tibetan name is *"bde ba 'phrul bkod."*

All-Encompassing Perfection - The Tibetan name is *"rdzogs pa spyi chings."*

Essence of Bodhicitta - The Tibetan name is *"byang chub sems tig."*

Infinite Bliss - The Tibetan name is *"bde ba rab 'byams."*

Wheel of Life - The Tibetan name is *"srog gi 'khor lo."*

Six Spheres - The Tibetan name is *"thig le drug pa."*

All-Penetrating Perfection - The Tibetan name is *"rdzogs pa spyi spyod."*

Wish-Fulfilling Jewel - The Tibetan name is *"yid bzhin nor bu."*

All-Unifying Pure Presence - The Tibetan name is *"kun tu rig pa."*

Supreme Lord - The Tibetan name is *"rje btsan dam pa."*

The Realization of the True Meaning of Meditation - The Tibetan name is *"sgom pa don grub."*

Kulayarāja Tantra

The Marvelous Primordial State - The Tibetan name is *"byang chub kyi sems rmad du byung ba."*

Let us discuss two of the above eighteen tantras to get a glimpse into the texts of Dzogchen practice.

The Cuckoo of Presence - The Tibetan name of this Semde tantra is *"rig pa'i khu byug."* The Cuckoo of Presence deals with the Six Vajra Verses. In ancient Tibetan culture, the cuckoo was considered a magical bird and the king of all fowls. Also, the cuckoo's first song heralds the coming of spring.

Therefore, the Six Vajra Verses of the Cuckoo of Presence tantra stands for the "Total-Presence of the Natural-Order of Mind Itself." This tantra is believed to be the root text of Dzogchen. This tantra deals with the idea that all of nature represents the non-dual divinity and the perfect purity in essence.

It teaches practitioners to accept this purity "as it is" without forming any conceptual conjectures because it is already self-perfected. Therefore, there is no need for any struggle to achieve any further perfection. This non-dual perfect purity is also on display and represents the Timeless Good. Just "being" is the natural order of things and is the basis of spontaneous contemplation.

Great Garuda in Flight - The Tibetan name is *"khyung chen lding ba."* The Tibetan name is "rtsal chen sprug pa." In Tibetan Buddhism, the garuda is associated with the "*khyung*," an important set of deities belonging to the Bon tradition. They are symbolically used in healing rituals to counter sicknesses caused by snakes or Nagas, as they are called in the Tibetan language.

In Dzogchen's teaching, the garuda is a manifestation of our primordial nature which is perfect and complete in all respects. The chicks of the garuda have their wings fully developed inside the egg itself. However, they cannot fly out until the egg hatches. The chicks have to wait for the shell to crack open before they can soar in flight.

The Dzogchen masters tell us that, in the same way, each of us has a fully-developed Buddhahood within us. It is veiled by the body, and when the body is discarded, the radiance of Buddhahood will shine.

The Four Yogas of Semde

The Semde teachings prescribe four yogas, namely:

Samatha - Samatha is a Buddhist term that can be translated as "tranquility of the mind" or "calm mindedness." It is believed that Shakyamuni identified two extremely important mental qualities that arise from meditation, both of which are crucial to achieving nirvana.

One of the two mental qualities is Samatha, and the other is "Vipasyana" or "Vipassana," which translates to "insight." The Tibetan word for Samatha is "shyine," which refers to the pacification of the mind and thoughts. Samatha is achieved through single-pointed meditation. Multiple mind-calming techniques are prescribed in Dzogchen to achieve Samatha.

Vipaśyanā - Also called Vipassana, this quality of mind refers to insight. This form of meditation helps seekers understand the "true nature of reality", as defined in Buddhism as suffering, unsatisfactoriness, and emptiness or sunyata.

Samatha and Vipassana go hand in hand, and one without the other will not help practitioners in any way. According to Buddhism, there are three ways one can achieve arhantship (authentic insight into the true nature of world phenomena), including:

- One can achieve calm abiding and then obtain insight
- One can achieve insight and then get abiding calm
- One can achieve insight and abiding calm together in tandem

The other two yogas are unbounded wholeness and spontaneous presence, both of which are discussed in a bit of detail in another chapter. These four yogas are parallel to the Four Yogas of Mahamudra.

A Dzogchen Prayer to the Guru

Homage to you! The primordial and supreme holder of the three kayas, father of all buddhas, great beacon of light.

Homage to you, Lokeswara, the Lord of the World! The brilliant moon of love and compassion is fondly looking after all beings. It is an ocean of inspiration and wisdom.

Homage to you, O Nangsi Zilnon, ruler of all that exists and appears, glorious Lotus-born buddha, holder of the treasury of wisdom and knowledge, taking on multiple appearances of multiple benevolent kings.

Homage to you, Pema Jungne, the Lotus-Born! You are the Vajra-lord because you were born from the Vajra. You are the Vajra king of Great Bliss.

Chapter 6: Longde Teachings

Longde or Space series teachings is one of the three scriptural divisions of Dzogchen. The term "longde" translates into "Space Series" or "Space Division." It emphasizes the concept of "emptiness" or "spaciousness" in the primordial natural state. The meditation methods in longde teachings facilitate removing all doubts that practitioners may have concerning the natural state.

Explaining Longde teachings is quite a difficult thing to do. First, it has fewer texts as compared to Semde. Also, it is quite abstract and can be learned only through experience. Describing what Longde teachings are is like describing the taste of coffee to someone who has never tasted it before.

Here's another analogy. To explain and describe a French dish to an Englishman, how would you do it? You don't go into the ingredients, right? Instead, you talk about the experience and how sweet, salty, or spicy the dish tastes and feels. You talk about the dish in such a way that the Englishman wants to taste it.

Even singing or playing a musical instrument is like this. When you hear someone singing beautifully or playing an instrument really well, you feel so moved that you want to learn and try to sing too. You also want to learn the musical instrument you just heard.

Singing and music are so beautiful that they communicate with a part of you that seems beyond your mind. That is the power of music, and it is enough to get you into the learning path. You like it, and you don't understand why you like it.

Longde teachings can be similarly understood. It describes Dzogchen practice and what can be expected as you go through the journey. You get hooked by this and choose to take the path. At the start of the journey, you really don't understand why you like it. The actual journey can be understood only when a convinced individual walks the path and learns and imbibes the teachings.

What is Emptiness or Shunyata?

According to Buddhism, *emptiness* (or shunyata) is not equal to *nothingness.* It is more like the Zero in mathematics. Interestingly, both the philosophical concept of shunyata and the mathematical concept of zero originated in India. In mathematics, zero appears to have no value, and yet it is the foundation of mathematics. The presence of the concept of zero leads to infinite numbers. For example, 10, 20, 30, etc., are possible only because zero exists.

In the same way, emptiness is not valueless. It is not "nothing." It is the basis of Buddhism. Emptiness means "empty of independent existence." This means that phenomena and all things do exist. Existence of any and all things can be only in two mutually exclusive ways, namely independent existence and dependent existence.

All things and phenomena that we experience are dependent on many things, including causes, conditions, etc. Therefore, there is no independent existence of all phenomena. This lack of independent existence is called sunyata or emptiness. Emptiness and dependent origination (this term and the twelve links are explained in detail in a different chapter of this book) are both sides of the same coin.

Because we live in the illusion of dependent origination, there is no independent existence. When we give up the illusion of dependent origin, then sunyata or emptiness can be experienced.

Samantabhadra's Royal Tantra of All-Inclusive Vastness

Also referred to as the "king" of tantras, Samantabhadra's Royal Tantra of All-Inclusive Vastness lists all the texts of Longde teachings. The texts of the Space Series include:

- King of Infinite Vast Space' or "Longchen Rabjam Gyalpo"
- Total Space of Samantabhadra' or "Kunto Zangpo Namkhache" or
- Manifestation of the Creative Energy of Pure Presence or "Rigpa Rangtsal Sharwa"
- Wheel of Key Instructions or "Dam-ngag Natshog Khorlo"
- Array of the Exalted Path or "Phaglam Kodpa"
- Vajrasattva Equal to the Limits of Space or "Dorje Sempa Namkha'i Thatang Nyampa"
- Secret Pristine Awareness or "Lamp of Secret Pristine Awareness" or "Yeshe Sangwa Dronma"
- Wheel of Precious Gems or "Rinpoche Khorlo"
- Secret Pristine Awareness or "Yeshe Sangwa"
- Perfect Pristine Awareness or "Yeshe Dzogpa"
- Total Revelation of the All-Pervasive State of Pure and Total Presence or "Changchub Kyi Sems Kunla Jugpa Namtag Tonpa"
- Radiant Vajra of the State of Pure and Total Presence or "Changchug Kyi Sem Dorje Odthro"

Setting up a daily meditation practice in Dzogchen is all about sitting in a quiet, undisturbed place to observe your thoughts as they start, rise, and cease. According to Dzogchen, all of us already have pure awareness embedded in us. In reality, there are no results to look for. So, one thing to do before beginning Dzogchen practice is to stop looking for results. Just be! Other simple tips for beginning living the life of Dzogchen practice include:

- Give up as much of your desires as you can
- Give up the need to have instant gratification and accept that cause and effect take their time to create the right condition for outcomes
- Stop watching TV excessively
- Stop discussing politics
- Stop buying and hoarding stuff. Learn to be happy with what you have. Here is a classic example of giving up your desires one at a time. If a new mobile phone has been released, remind yourself you don't need a new one. The old one is good enough for your needs. Don't buy it
- Live a simple and frugal life. Don't overindulge when it comes to food and clothing

All the above elements of modern life enhance illusions and delusions, taking you further away from your inherent goodness. Therefore, before even starting meditation techniques, learn to live like a hermit amid the modern world to the best extent possible.

In today's world, giving up desires becomes even more imperative than before. The world is changing so much and so fast that before we get hold of one of our desires, the next one pops up, making our life an overflowing but bottomless pit of worldly desires. The more we put in, the deeper the pit gets.

Also, the amount of information available globally is so much that the human mind finds it difficult to catch up. Consequently, the confusions and conflicts in our minds enhance the obscurations hiding the inherent goodness we all already possess.

We end up mindlessly chasing for things we believe will give us "happiness." This is where Dzogchen comes to our aid. This ancient practice says there is no need to chase happiness because it is already there within each of us. In fact, "doing" something is counterproductive to happiness. We just need to stay with our afflictive emotions and thoughts so the confusion muddying our mind settles down and we get clarity.

Desires, the cause of all suffering, are the primary elements that muddy the mind preventing you from achieving clarity. Only when you live a simple, contented life with what you have, keeping your desires minimalistic, can you look for enlightenment using Dzogchen meditation techniques. If your desires and needs don't cease, then it does not matter how regular you are with your meditation practices. You are unlikely to move forward in the path of knowing and identifying pure awareness.

Sky Meditation

The need for meditation comes alive when the desire to release conflicts and entanglements from our minds takes seed. We feel like meditating when we want to give up the notion of "self" hoping we will find elusive happiness. Meditation, in Dzogchen, is about doing nothing but acknowledging and accepting one moment at a time along with the experiences and verbal thoughts that moment brings with it.

Meditation is about being aware of each moment and identifying the pleasure, pain, thoughts, and conflicts it brings. Without identifying with these elements, we can simply rest in the awareness of them, which allows us to go beyond the conditions, which, in turn, helps us connect with the lightness of our hearts. Meditation helps us practice the art of resting in awareness. The more we practice, the more our powers of focus and concentration increase leading to clarity of our minds.

The first step in meditation, after being seated comfortably, is to take note of our body and mind. What is the current state of your mind and body? Are you distracted, angry, resentful, happy, comfortable, peaceful, worried, excited? Observing your state of body and mind, take a couple of deep breaths, and relax. Give space for all the findings of your mind as you sit down to meditate.

This space of acceptance becomes your foundation to use the powerful and transformative power of your attention flexibly. Mindfulness meditation techniques help us zoom in on one particular event or thought. This "zooming" capability of our mind is a great tool to stabilize our meditation practice with close-up attention.

The "close-up" attention, for a beginner, is usually to focus on the breath or on one's thoughts at that precise moment. With practice, an accomplished practitioner will become so absorbed in his or her meditation that the subject and object will merge into one and disappear.

You will begin to realize that you become your breath. You become the tingling on your feet, the thoughts and emotions, and you become the sadness or joy you bring into yourself. Entanglement in our lives and with our ego slowly but surely *reduces*. Our fears and hopes dissolve, and our sense of self gets lost. In fact, with a little bit of practice, you will notice you find it easy to become so absorbed that you lose your sense of self during the meditation session.

You identify and understand how the entire experience of your world is impermanent, ungraspable, and temporary. At some point in time, through this understanding, wisdom can manifest itself to you.

And yet, often, while we are meditating with close-up attention, an unnecessary sense of struggle exists between focusing between overlapping thoughts or ideas that can be created. Therefore, it is better to find a vaster and more open space for our attention. To give you an analogy, suppose you are walking on the road. It is impossible to focus only on your breath or thought while doing so. You could miss the traffic signal or bump into others walking around you, resulting in increased confusion defeating the very purpose of meditation. So, we need to expand the space of our awareness from one moment to a mid-range level.

During meditation, we expand our focus of attention from just our breath to include the entire energy experience of our body as we breathe. In the same way, when we walk, we can increase our awareness range to include the sights, smells, and other sensory experiences around us. In such a situation, it is considered that our awareness "sits on our shoulders." Our attention has a wise perspective in this state, identifying and acknowledging each event, moment, and thought with compassion and humility.

Slowly but surely, as you practice this meditation, you will find it easy to let go of the illusion of "getting somewhere" in each moment. Instead, you just stay in the moment, savoring everything it throws at you, resting in your current awareness. You will soon realize there is nothing to be and nothing to have.

This mid-level range of meditation expanse might also not serve the purpose of achieving pure awareness. Often, you get stuck in an endless loop of repetitive thoughts or events in your mind. Also, there could be noise and chaos around preventing you from achieving calmness of mind.

In such a circumstance, we allow our awareness to open up fully and become like the sky. Buddha taught, "Develop a mind like the vastness of limitless space. In this space, allow all good and bad, pleasant and unpleasant experiences to come together without conflict or struggle and then disappear. Think of your mind as a vast sky and rest in it without struggle."

With this wide, vast perspective, we can sit or walk in our meditation. We open our attention to allowing all experiences to enter without a sense of boundary. We should let go of our mind, which appears to be contained in our body, and experience its unbounded vastness. This is Sky Meditation.

All three types of meditation should be practiced according to need. Our awareness is highly flexible, and these meditation techniques help increase its flex even more. Every form of awareness is liberating. The more liberated you feel, the less dependent on "existence" your life will be.

Chapter 7: Menngagde Teachings

Also called "oral transmission," the Menngagde teachings are transmitted orally where the master and student sit opposite each other. The master "tells" and "talks" to the student about the true nature of reality and shows him or her the path to achieve realization.

The Menngagde Series, which focuses on rigpa, is also referred to as the "Secret Instruction Series of Dzogchen teachings and is divided into two sections, namely Trekcho and Togal. Trekcho or "Kadag Trekcho" deals with "cutting through solidity related to primordial purity." Togal or Lhundrun Togal is about the "direct crossing of spontaneous presence."

The Menngagde teachings discuss successive reflections called the "seven lojong" or the "seven mind training." Sri Singha divided the Menngagde teachings into four further divisions, which include:
- Outer Cycle
- Inner Cycle
- Secret Cycle
- Innermost Unexcelled Cycle

The fourth and the last division of Menngagde teachings contain the seventeen tantras. Let us begin the Menngagde teachings by understanding the Seven Mind Training.

Seven Mind Training

There are seven points of mind training. And each point takes one a step closer to realization. Let us look at them in a bit of detail.

The Preliminaries

This is the first step in preparing yourself in the preliminaries before taking the leap into the Dzogchen practice. The preliminaries consist of three contemplations:

- Contemplation of the difficulty of finding advantages and freedoms
- Contemplation on impermanence and death
- Contemplations on the trials of samsara

The Main Practice

There are two parts to training in bodhicitta (or enlightenment) including:

- Training in absolute or ultimate bodhicitta
- Training in relative bodhicitta.

Training in ultimate bodhicitta has three sets of practices, namely the preparation, the primary part, and the conclusion. At the preparation stage, take refuge and generate bodhicitta. Pray to the deity and master and offer seven branches. Then sit down for meditation in an upright position and breathe in and out 21 times, ensuring your confusions and mental activities are calmed down. With this, you become like a vessel ready to receive the power of meditative concentration.

Here are some pointers as to how you can practice in ultimate bodhicitta training.

Treat all your experiences and all the phenomena you see around you as a dream. Consider them as being dreamlike.

- Examine the nature of the unborn awareness that is inherent in all sentient beings.
- Free the antidote also from its place.
- Rest in the Alaya of habits.
- Between meditation sessions, consider yourself to be a conjurer of illusions.

Meditate and bring awareness to the three objects, three poisons, and the three sources of virtue. Practice all activities by applying slogans and prayers.

Training in relative bodhicitta has two parts, namely meditation and post-meditation. Here are some pointers for the meditation part:

Train in giving – taking, alternately. Both are essential in all aspects of life. Giving and taking are rooted in the most basic human activity, namely breathing. We take in and give out in breathing. Therefore, in other aspects of human life, too, we must give as well as take. Some quotes of Acharya Shantideva that reiterate the importance of giving and taking:

Unless you can give your happiness for others' suffering, you will not get the enlightenment you seek. You will also not find happiness in samsara.

If you wish to protect yourself and others, then you must practice the secret mystery of exchanging yourself for others.

In the relative bodhicitta meditation, you must start with your mother in this birth who gave birth to you to learn about and practice Buddha's teachings. Be grateful to your mother for this opportunity. Then, you want to give back something in return for her kindness. The best thing you can do is to help her end samsaric suffering.

What can benefit your mother? Happiness and virtue. Therefore, give away all your happiness and virtue to her. Generate thoughts in your head that through this accumulation of merit, your mother will achieve enlightenment. Do the same thing for your father too.

Slowly include all sentient beings in your meditation. Take in all their sufferings and give out all your happiness and virtue. This giving and taking are rooted in breathing. Therefore, breathe out all your virtue and happiness and breathe in all their suffering.

In the post-meditation, contemplate three types of objects, three poisons, and three sources of virtue. Three types of objects include pleasant, unpleasant, and neutral. We experience three emotions or poisons through these types, namely attachment, aversion, and dullness, respectively. Many beings experience the effects of these three poisons.

Here, we contemplate taking all the three poisons from other people, thereby freeing them from the three objects. This, in turn, results in them gaining three sources of virtue without attachment, aversion, and dullness.

Mindfulness is an important aspect of post-meditation. This means you must recite slogans such as, "May all the vices and negative actions of others come onto me and ripen in me. May all my happiness and virtues go onto them and ripen there."

With this, you will feel an intense resolve to take on others' sufferings. To this end, we must also take on our future sufferings in the present to make ourselves capable of bearing others' suffering.

Transforming Challenges and Adversity into the Path of Realization or Enlightenment

When you believe that the world is full of evil or that your life is full of rife, train your mind to convert every challenge and adversity into a path of enlightenment. Blame no one or just allow the feelings of blame to disappear into the vast sky of your awareness.

When unwholesome actions become excessive, natural resources begin to deplete, sentient beings become unruly, and many negative effects can be seen. When such forms of adversity come up, then they can be converted into the path of enlightenment through action and intention.

Intention has two parts:
- Transforming adversity into the path of enlightenment through ultimate bodhicitta
- Transforming adversity into the path of enlightenment through relative bodhicitta

Through relative bodhicitta - Before we began living the life of Dharma, we did not realize that suffering is caused through self-grasping. We also did not recognize the kindness and compassion of sentient beings. Instead, we blamed them for our suffering. Now that we know that all suffering is rooted in self-grasping, we must learn to drive blame into that one aspect alone, our self-grasping. Here is a powerful quote that explains the significance of knowing and acknowledging the concept of self-grasping:

If all the fears, sufferings, and harm are derived only through self-clinging or self-grasping, then why do you need to hold on to this? Let go of it and liberate yourself from suffering.

The realization that, from the dawn of time, we have clung to a non-existent self, and to maintain this illusion, we have accumulated karma resulting in limitless births and rebirths, is the beginning of the journey of realization. Here is another verse is taken from the book "Introduction to Bodhisattva's Way of Life" to explain how our mind clings to the non-existent self:

O mind, you have lived eons and centuries of life,

Clinging onto an illusory self, pursuing your self-interests,

And despite all your efforts,

You have seen nothing but misery and suffering.

It is, therefore, important to treat this self-grasping as your enemy that stands in the way of being liberated from samsara suffering. Whenever you examine yourself when you feel the effects of self-grasping, the examination of the self will demonstrate to you its absence. Use this prayer to keep the effects of self-grasping at bay:

There was a time when you could hide and harm me,

Now, that time has passed.

I can see you clearly for what you are.

I will crush you and your power over me.

Subjugating this demon will take you far in the journey of Dzogchen. People are divided into different categories depending on their intentions and actions. Sentient beings who direct their intentions and actions towards their own well-being are called "laymen" in the language of Buddhism. Those who direct their intentions and actions for the benefit of others are called Dharma practitioners.

And finally, meditate and focus on the compassion and kindness of all beings. Generally, all beings have been kind to us from the start. Buddha said this of laypeople:

> *Given that attaining Buddhahood depends on both ordinary beings and buddhas, it does not make sense to honor only the buddhas and not respect and revere ordinary beings who, in turn, have the potential to become Buddhas. Therefore, meditate on the kindness and compassion of all beings.*

If you are keen on attaining Buddhahood, then sentient beings and buddhas are equal when it comes to their kindness and compassion. Therefore, we must cultivate love and compassion for ordinary beings. We must take on their suffering and give them our happiness and virtue so we are prepared and ready to receive enlightenment at the end of the journey.

Through ultimate bodhicitta - Meditate on the illusions you experience as the four kayas are protected by sunyata or emptiness. The concept of sunyata is discussed in detail in a later chapter in this book. Apply the fourfold practice in all your life experiences and encounters.

Let us try and understand the four kayas. According to Dzogchen, whenever we experience suffering and/or mental afflictions from the outer world, those sufferings are also delusions and illusionary constructs of our minds. These elements do not even have a trace of existence. These appearances can be compared to a dream which disappears as soon as you wake up from it. Every delusionary appearance can be described in terms of the four kayas, namely:

- Since it is illusionary and does not originate from anywhere, it is considered the unborn dharmakaya
- If it has not risen, then it cannot cease, and therefore, it is the unceasing sambhogakaya
- If anything that does not arise or cease, then it cannot have an interim. Therefore, it is non-abiding nirmanakaya
- And it has an indivisible essence; it is svabhavikakaya

When you view and meditate on all your delusionary appearances as the four kayas (or buddha-bodies), you are practicing the instruction on how to recognize and identify the four kayas.

Interestingly, Buddhism treats even those elements that harm us as being kind to us. The belief is that those that harm us are the very ones that drive us to train in the two types of bodhicitta. The more harm we endure, the more we want to end it. The need to end harm and suffering is the starting point of the Dzogchen journey.

Action is the practice of accumulation and purification that helps in transforming adversity into the path of enlightenment. The fourfold practice is considered to be the best method of action.

The Practice of Accumulating Merit - Whenever we feel suffering, and it is natural and common to think to ourselves, "It would be so wonderful for this suffering to end and happiness to begin." This thought should trigger the action to accumulate merit because "to be happy without suffering is possible only when we accumulate merit." Here are some ways to accumulate merit:
- Make offerings to your master or lama or guru
- Respect and venerate the Sangha
- Offer tormas to elemental spirits

Basically, we must do such actions so that we gather merit verbally, physically, and mentally. Our prayers must not be beseeching of a good life. Instead, our prayers should be one of submission. Here is an example, "If it is better that I learn to escape from suffering by being sick, then let me be sick. If, however, I am better being healed, then let me be healed. And if it is better that I die, then grant me death."

The practice of purifying negative actions - Abandoning the cause of suffering is the way to end it. Ending the cause of suffering is by way of purifying negative actions. We must feel repentance for our past mistakes. We must vow never to repeat those mistakes again, even at the cost of our lives. Repentance and restraint are admirable purifying tools.

Then we take refuge in the dharma and generate bodhicitta, recite special mantras, and meditate on emptiness; all of these antidotes are used to correct and purify our negative actions. We must confess our sins through the four powers of repentance, restraint, taking support from dharma, and antidotal action.

The Practice of Offering to Harmful Influences - You must offer prayers and tormas to harmful influences because they are why your desire to end suffering has come. The prayers would go something like this, "You are kind and compassionate because you support my journey to achieve enlightenment. Pass on all the sufferings of others onto me."

Another way to offer prayers to harmful influences is to cultivate loving-kindness towards them. You can command them with the prayer, "With whatever I do for you now and in the long term, do not come in the way of my dharma practice."

The Practice of Offering to Dharma Protectors - Offer prayers and tormas to dharma protectors seeking their help in pacifying beings and elements that might stand in the way of your dharma. Pray to them to create favorable conditions for you to practice the dharma.

Applying the Dzogchen Practice Right Through Your Life

The essence of the Dzogchen practice is to apply yourself to the five strengths. Also, the Mahayana instructs that the same five strengths are needed for the transference of power and enlightenment. Good conduct throughout our life is essential. The five strengths are:

The strength of impetus - This impetus is to strengthen the mind by repeatedly thinking the following thought: "From this moment, this month, this year onwards, and for the rest of my life, I will be separated from the two kinds of bodhicitta."

The strength of familiarization - This strength is to repeatedly train in the two forms of bodhicitta.

The strength of wholesome seeds - This strength is all about accumulating merit as much as possible so that bodhicitta grows and develops.

The strength of revulsion - This strength is to help you reflect on the cause and effects of suffering, should self-cherishing thoughts create obstacles on the path of enlightenment. This strength calls for repeated self-reminders of the harmful effects of desires and negative actions and how they drive sentient beings away from dharma. These repeated reminders will give you the strength of revulsion so you can throw out self-cherishing thoughts from your life.

The strength of aspiration - For this, after every virtuous deed, you must make an aspiration like, "From now on until I achieve realization, let me not be separated from the two bodhicitta. May I be able to convert every adversity into a path of enlightenment and let it support my journey."

These five strengths together constitute a practice that brings everything together within a single "hum." The same five strengths are the instructions to follow at the moment of death too. Whenever a dharma practitioner gets so sick they are sure to die, the practice of wholesome seeds would be to hand over all their possessions to the greatest source of merit.

The strength of aspiration is to offer seven branches to the master with a prayer. For example, "Bless me so that during the bardo (the space-time continuum between death and rebirth) and future rebirths, I may continue to train in the two bodhicitta. Bless me so that I may meet my master or guru in the future birth for this purpose."

The strength of revulsion in this circumstance would be thoughts such as, "Self-cherishing thoughts resulted in a lot of suffering in the past, and they will do so unless I am freed from them. I have examined this body and realized that the self is the most graspable thing in the body and mind." This final prayer will help in freeing the practitioner from self-grasping.

The strength of impetus is to cultivate the intention repeatedly so the practitioner continues to train in twofold bodhicitta even in the bardo.

The Measure of Mind Training

All teachings have a single purpose: to lead sentient beings to enlightenment by taming self-grasping. The primary purpose of dharma is to be an antidote to self-grasping. There are two witnesses to all phenomena, namely yourself and the beings outside of you.

Meeting or not meeting other people's approval might or might not be a testimony to the righteousness of your dharma path. Ordinary beings are not capable of reading your mind. They can only glimpse at the true version of any practitioner based on his or her outer conduct. So, it is possible that you "pretend" to walk on the path of dharma. At the same time, you continue to do the wrong things, although surreptitiously.

Therefore, you must examine your own mind because you are the reliable witness for your intentions and actions. Remember to always rely on the reliable one. Examine your mind, honestly. There is no need for shame or guilt if you encounter negative thoughts and actions. Just find and implement the antidote and move on in your path authentically.

Always keep a positive, joyful attitude. When you do this, even if you get distracted from the focus on Dzogchen practice, you will be proficient.

The Commitments of Mind Training

Train continuously in the three basic principles, which include:
- Not to stray from the commitments of mind training - in addition, you must learn and practice all the lesser precepts of Vajrayana too, and not allow them to decline.
- Not to be careless and reckless - This trap is easy to fall into, especially if you want to demonstrate to others that you have no self-cherishing thoughts. Avoid this attitude and practice dharma genuinely and with true intention.

- Not to fall into the trap of partiality - You must avoid all forms of partiality. It is easy to respect a powerful person and disrespect a weak person. This kind of partial behavior must be avoided.

Be prepared to change your attitude from self-cherishing to cherishing others around you. However, always remain neutral. Don't talk about injured limbs, which means you should not point out other people's flaws.

Start training with your hardest and most difficult afflictive emotion, and then move in decreasing order of difficulty. Give up all expectations of outcomes and results for any and all of your actions.

Avoid being excessively loyal to any cause. Avoid lashing out in retaliation to anyone, even if that person behaves badly with you. Don't hit or take advantage of anyone's vulnerable point. Don't hide and wait to ambush. Let your behavior be open and transparent.

Don't transfer the burden from one person to another. Carry what is yours. Avoid competitive behavior. Do your best at all times, regardless of the expected outcomes. Take care while performing prescribed rites and rituals. Do not perform them wrongly, don't bring gods to the level of demons, and do not use other's weaknesses to your advantage.

The Precepts of Mind Training

Do everything with the single intention of benefiting as many people as you can. Counter all your problems with one remedy: to accept everything happening in your life with equanimity.

You should live your life based on two tasks, one at the beginning and the second at the end. Initially, this would translate into starting each day with the right impetus, "Today, I shall not be separated from the two bodhicitta." Maintain this awareness right through the day. In the end, while examining your day's activities, if you find faults, then accept them, confess to them, and resolve not to repeat them.

If you become rich and famous, don't allow them to cause arrogance in you. Instead, identify and recognize the illusionary aspect of your seemingly prosperous life and use your advantages to benefit others. If, on the other hand, you become so destitute and poor that you have access to nothing more than water, recognize that the state is illusionary. Do not be discouraged by your hardships.

You have to keep two things even at the cost of your life. These two things are the commitments of dharma, in general, and the commitment to mind training, in particular. If you let go of even one of these two, then you can jeopardize the happiness of your own future.

Avoid the six misunderstandings, which include:
- **Misplaced patience** - When you have the patience to outdo an enemy and protect your friend but don't have the patience to follow the dharma, it is misplaced patience.
- **Misplaced intention** - To take an interest in the riches and glory of leading a life of dharma but have no interest in pure Dharma practice.
- **Misplaced relish** - To enjoy the taste of the worldly pleasures provided by dharma but have no taste for the study, reflection, and meditation as prescribed by dharma.
- **Misplaced compassion** - If you fail to have compassion for the wrongdoers but end up feeling kind and compassionate towards the followers of dharma, you are guilty of misplaced compassion. Every being deserves to be treated with compassion.
- **Misplaced pursuit** - If you do not encourage your dependents to pursue the practice of dharma but encourage them to increase the riches and glories of this life, then you are practicing misplaced pursuit.

- **Misplaced joy** - The failure to cultivate joy for the virtues and happiness of samsara and nirvana but end up being happy when rivals fail

The seven-mind training is long and elaborate. It makes sense to take one at a time and practice and perfect each slowly but surely.

Chapter 8: Getting Ready for Dzogchen

Compassion and wisdom are essential to achieve enlightenment or awareness. There are three broad types of mindsets, namely inferior, mediocre, and superior. Within each, there are three types, namely:
- Inferior inferior, inferior mediocre, inferior superior
- Mediocre inferior, mediocre mediocre, mediocre superior
- Superior inferior, superior mediocre, superior superior

These are all general types, theoretically speaking. In reality, there is an infinite number of mindsets because there is an infinite number of ways we can think (or not think). Some people are very compassionate, some moderately compassionate, and others have little compassion. In the same way, levels of wisdom are also infinite in number. Therefore, different levels of teaching are needed to find something that suits each individual's personality, mindset, and thinking process.

According to Dzogchen, teachings can come in different and unconventional methods, not just through written texts or discourses, which we have to read, understand, and practice. Enlightenment can come in various forms. For example, there is a story of a Dzogchen master who was traveling with two of his students.

They reached a river bank and decided to spend the night there. As they were lying on the ground, the master asked some questions of his students. "Do you see the stars?"

"Yes, master," they replied.

"Do you hear the barking of dogs?"

"Yes, master," they replied. As the students answered these questions posed by their master, they learned about the nature of the mind. Most of us know the answers to these questions. But often, the right moment, the right question, the right environment, and the right master come together to spark off (a click, as it were) the moment of enlightenment.

This concept might seem difficult for a beginner to understand. You might ask, "Is this really possible? That we learn awareness in a click?" According to Dzogchen, this is possible because awareness is already within your mind. The clutter covering this awareness needs to be removed, and that's all. This can happen in a moment shared between a dedicated student and a learned master.

This awareness can come about by pondering simple questions such as "seeing stars" or "hearing the sound of dogs barking," which are not really found in complex texts. In fact, it is possible to spend years meditating and reading complex texts and still not find enlightenment. The reason for this is usually the practitioner's own obscuration. Obscuration relates to ignorance and the idea of clinging or attachment to all phenomena. We find it difficult to let go and simply allow everything to be "as it is." When the student, helped by his or her master, can break down this obscuration, he or she achieves enlightenment.

When we cling to all internal and external phenomena, then it gives rise to duality. Duality is the prime cause of all the aggression and desire we feel. Ignorance-wrapped duality causes obscurations.

We must purify and eliminate all these obscurations to see, identify, and realize our basic goodness or awareness.

The method to purify the obscurations and eliminate passions, aggressions, and desires gives rise to wisdom. According to Dzogchen, 84,000 passions need to be purified, pacified, and transmuted. The condensed teachings that help this purification of obscurations are categorized into three baskets: vinaya, sutra, and Abhidharma. Hinayana, Mahayana, Vajrayana, etc., are also called baskets of teachings.

And finally, you get to the Dzogchen practice to see and realize the true nature of reality or primordial awareness or rigpa. Buddha is considered kind and compassionate. No one before or after him has given us teachings with so many varied levels that cater to all kinds of mindsets and personalities.

Training in the Preliminaries

Before you get into Dzogchen practice, you must train in the preliminaries, which consist of three contemplations, namely:
- On the difficulty of finding advantages and freedoms
- On impermanence and death
- On the trials of samsara

Freedom and Advantages - First, you must think of how fortunate you are to have accumulated enough merit to get a human life. Then think about the advantage and freedom of having the support to practice the Dharma. Both of these by themselves are abundant virtues.

Even those born as humans with inherent pure awareness don't get the support or pathway to practice the Dharma. When we contemplate other life forms such as animals and insects, we feel grateful for human life.

Now that we have rare advantages and freedom, we must not waste it. We must use this life effectively and practice Dharma.

Death and Impermanence - Meditate and contemplate on life and realize how uncertain life is. Death can come in any form when the conditions of the karmic cycle are met. Therefore, we must put all our energies into the sacred Dzogchen practice immediately.

The Trials of Samsara - Contemplate the teachings where you learn that vices and unwholesome actions result in pleasure and pain. Both are temporary and only increase the craving in our minds. Practice virtue as much as possible.

Importance of Samatha and Vipassana Meditation

Buddha broadly divided his myriad teachings into two broad types, namely relative teachings and absolute teachings. The teachings help practitioners deal with the process of meditation and post-meditation stages in the Mahayana, Theravada. Mahamudra, and Dzogchen levels. Finally, there will come the point when practitioners do not distinguish between meditation and post-meditation stages, and this level is the highest in Dzogchen.

With some practice, it is possible to have some level of awareness or at least glimpses of awareness during meditation. But to maintain this state in the post-meditation stage is quite difficult unless you are grounded and connected with your innate awareness. Without this, it will not be possible to realize the meditation and post-meditation non-distinguishable stage.

Without being grounded to your awareness, your mind will flutter between thoughts, just like how a piece of paper will flutter wherever the wind takes it. Therefore, the practice of Samatha meditation is crucial in all forms of Buddhist practice, including Dzogchen. Samatha meditation is all about stabilizing the mind, after which pristine awakening through vipassana, extraordinary insight is possible.

Vipassana outcomes are possible when the mind is calm and clear with Samatha outcomes.

A calm and clear mind is like a clear lake that has no muddy water. Just as you can see the fish, stones, and plants inside the lake when it is clear, you can have extraordinary insight into your mind when it is calm. An ungrounded and destabilized mind is constantly wavering, and in such a situation, you cannot have insight.

Meditation is how to bring the choppy, unstable mind into a state of stability and groundedness. Your meditation practice as taught to you by your chosen master should be the way forward. Specifically for Western countries, a stable mind is possible only when people look beyond the absurd, materialistic world they live in.

Meditation is extremely beneficial in such circumstances to help people deal with the stresses and anxieties of life situations. Daily meditation of at least half an hour is crucially important before moving ahead in your Dzogchen practice. This daily meditation practice is extremely useful in bringing peace, joy, and happiness into your life.

Conventional truth and Absolute or Unconventional Truth

All of Buddha's teachings can be categorized broadly into two baskets: conventional truth and absolute truth. Conventional truth is the path of cause and effect, while absolute or unconventional truth is about going beyond and above the path of cause and effect.

Buddhism emphasizes the middle path and does not support the view of extreme nihilism or eternalism. The nihilistic view looks at all phenomena as pure incidents and views everything as accidental. It does not believe in karma, cause and effect, birth, rebirth, good and bad, etc. Every phenomenon is a pure incident by itself. In Buddhism, a nihilistic view is seen as the lowest level because it leads one to darkness, ignorance, and suffering even as one becomes exceedingly attached to samsara.

On the other extreme is eternalism which Buddhism sees as being a better view than nihilism. Eternalism sees things as good and bad and uses morality to categorize behaviors and situations so that "bad" things can be avoided and "good" things can be embraced. And yet, extreme eternalism is also incorrect.

Eternalism also drives you to become attached to the "good" things. Also, such a view drives you to "hate" or "dislike" "bad" things, which is also a form of attachment. You end up holding on to phenomena which powers your ego. Another element of eternalism is that it often gives false hope to people by focusing excessively on the "good" and the "bad." Eternalism, therefore, fosters attachment and aggression, both of which are obscurations to enlightenment.

The middle path of Buddhism goes beyond nihilism and eternalism. This view is deeper than both nihilism and eternalism and more difficult to realize. The middle path also offers hope, just as eternalism does. However, the hope offered through this practice is genuine. It provides the path wherein every individual chooses what is best for them to achieve enlightenment, which is already inherent in all humans.

The Power of Our Ego

There is an interesting debate between Milarepa, a famous Buddhist master, and a scholar. The scholar once argued that space is open as well as movable. However, Milarepa used his powers to make the scholar immobile for a while to demonstrate that space is unmovable. This exercise was to eliminate and break the scholar's ego, who believed that he knew everything there is to know. Getting rid of one's ego is one of the primary prerequisites to achieving enlightenment.

Also, Milarepa's lesson to the scholar was that nothing could be labeled or categorized in any particular way. When we talk of everything as being this or that, we effectively promote duality and take extreme viewpoints. By taking extreme views of eternalism or nothingness, we miss out on the path of knowing and realizing the true nature of reality.

When we miss the true nature of reality, we are in an unnatural state of mind. A dualistic mind is unnatural. And in this unnatural state, there is obstruction and obscuration in mind. Consequently, the basic goodness inherent in you is blocked. In the same way, ego blocks our ability to connect with our natural goodness, which makes ego unnatural.

The ego plays a very powerful game in our lives. It confuses and confounds us. When the ego is allowed to have control over us, we live our life like a dream. We are always confused and muddled in our dreams, moving aimlessly from one scene to another. When you wake up, the dream is not there, right?

In the same way, when we become enlightened and wake up from the "dream" that we are unconsciously living in, we will notice that all phenomena are actually not there. Everything we experience and sense is a projection of our mind. And for this to happen, obscurations should be eliminated.

Sadly, we are so used to living and being in an unnatural state of mind we have come to believe it *is* natural and the other state is not. In many ways, it seems like the modern human, thanks to losing touch with this natural state of compassion and wisdom, has lost his mind.

Therefore, regardless of the path we choose, we are unlikely to achieve enlightenment unless we change our minds because the path is actually our mind. There is no path put by someone outside of you for you to walk on. Your mind is the path, and there is nothing outside of it. Everything is in it. So, you have to start your journey by deepening yourself so your mind grows and develops.

Forgiveness and Letting Go

To heal our minds, we must first let go of resentment, anger, and all other ego-related issues that hold us back from the path of reaching our basic goodness. Holding onto resentment and anger can be compared to a cat running around in circles trying in vain to catch its own tail. This exercise is not only futile but also makes your mind confused like a muddy lake.

Forgiving people is a great way to get rid of negative emotions from your mind and bring harmony into your life. This exercise will clear the muddle in your mind, and it will become clear like a clear lake through which you can have extraordinary insights.

For a beginner, starting at the Hinayana level might be a great idea because this teaching is focused on the growth and development of the individual. When as an individual, you have achieved enlightenment, then you can move on to helping others around you. The most basic and comprehensive teaching of Hinayana (or Lower Vehicle or teaching) is "not to harm any being."

The thought that encompasses all of Mahayana's teaching is "to benefit all beings." When we practice the concept of not harming any being, we automatically end up benefiting all beings. So, if you notice, the Hinayana path is contained in the Mahayana path. In this way, lower teachings are included in the higher teaching, whereas the reverse is not true.

Accumulation of Merit

Learning the Dzogchen practice depends a lot on the student's dedication coupled with the blessings of a master. The highest form of Buddhist wisdom can be bestowed on a willing and determined student by a master in just one sitting. It is possible that as a student, you might sit down as an ordinary being to listen to the teachings of your master. And when you get up, you could have achieved realization and become enlightened.

Of course, for a student to achieve enlightenment in just one sitting, he or she would have to reach "almost enlightenment." The student would have to prepare their mind until the spark is ready to be lit by the blessings of a master. This almost miraculous kind of event can happen to people with an enormous amount of merit. It is not likely to happen to people who lack any kind of merit.

So, any person to become enlightened would have to work at accumulating a lot of merit, of which there are two types, the conventional and unconventional. Conventional merit is all about doing what you can to use your physical and mental capacities to help people in all possible ways. Conventional merit is measured by six paramitas or "perfections" (in the same order as mentioned below), namely:
- "Dhan," a Sanskrit word that literally translates to "giving."
- Sheila - virtue
- Diligence
- Patience
- Samadhi
- Wisdom or "prajna"

Wisdom comes last only when the accumulation of merit in the five parameters is sufficient to take a practitioner to wisdom. Only when a sentient accumulates sufficient conventional merit is he or she ready to realize the basic goodness of nature already inherent in all sentient beings.

When a student is ready with accumulated merit, then he or she needs a lineage without which enlightenment is impossible. As mentioned before, the Dzogchen lineage is considered the highest teaching level in Tibetan Buddhism. The primary stage of Dzogchen practice is to recognize the true nature of the mind. Once practitioners achieve this level, they need to move on to the next, which calls for perfecting it.

Perfecting awareness differs greatly from getting glimpses of awareness which may or may not be achieved even by beginners. These glimpses of awareness are not sufficient to achieve stability of the mind.

Before a student gets introduced to the reality of their mind at the Dzogchen level, they must clearly see the mind for what it truly is. Perfecting Samatha meditation techniques to calm your mind takes a lot of time and effort.

For example, a student practicing meditation for several years will quickly and deeply achieve a calm state of mind. Someone who has had only a couple of weeks of practice will take a much longer time and effort to do so.

Just how any activity is perfected through continuous and relentless practice, meditation also has different levels such as beginner, intermediary, advanced, senior, etc. As you move from one level to another, you will see how much better you are getting at handling your mind. The mind is the same whether you are at a beginner or advanced, or any other level. The mind does not change. It's your capability to manage your mind that comes with practice and perfection.

Perfecting meditation techniques is what will help you realize your non-dual true awareness. When this state is reached, all emotions and hitherto "separate" phenomena will disappear into it. Everything, including emotions like aggression, jealousy, complex thoughts, and all else, is liberated. That liberating awareness purifies everything that comes in contact with it.

The most important concept of Dzogchen teaching is that awareness or rigpa is already inside of us. We just need to clear all the obscurations that obscure the awareness to realize its power.

Preparing for Dzogchen through various levels of meditation and accumulating merit helps to get rid of all obscuration.

Ngondro Teachings

This teaching has two parts, namely inner Ngondro and outer Ngondro. The inner Ngondro deals with the training of the mind to get detached from the unending samsara. A prayer for this mind training goes something like this:

> *I prostrate and thank the lama, the embodiment of the three kayas. I pray to the lama that I make my precious human birth worthwhile. I have received this precious human body by accumulating an immense amount of positive karma to be born as a human being. Please help me make it worthwhile.*
>
> *I know samsara is full of suffering. Please bless me so that I don't get trapped in this place of suffering for long and that I achieve enlightenment. Bless me to turn my mind away from this suffering and its causes. Bless me so that I don't follow a life of suffering rooted in ceaseless and insatiable desires.*

The four outer Ngondro teachings often start with a week of training the mind to know, understand, and appreciate the importance of the precious human life we are born in. Students meditate on the impermanence of life. Death is certain. We all know we are going to die, and yet we waste our precious human lives getting increasingly trapped in the sufferings of the samsara. We could die the next minute, yet we are planning for tomorrow when Dzogchen students meditate on this concept of impermanence before they move to Dzogchen teaching.

Chapter 9: How to Awaken Your Rigpa

Dzogchen Meditation focuses on the following three activities, in the same order:

- Accessing and identifying the Alaya of habits
- The effulgent rigpa
- The essence rigpa

Recognizing the Alaya of Habits

What is Alaya? Buddhism defines it as an eternal matter or substance that creates and is contained in all forms and phenomena. When you see it in its entirety, it is non-existing. However, when you see it as part of all phenomena, it appears everywhere and fills the cosmos.

It appears to be the nature of all worldly things. It is the storehouse of relative and absolute consciousness. It is defined as the fundamental mind-consciousness of sentient beings and holds all the experiences of an individual's life. Seeing, hearing, imagining, etc., are all formed in the Alaya of habits which, in turn, gives rise to labeling "this" and "that."

Recognizing the Alaya of habits goes way beyond conceptual mental cognition, which deals with our physical and mental senses, and our ability to discern and label all the phenomena we see and experience in our lives. The Alaya of habits goes deeper than the recognition of milliseconds of non-conceptual hearing and seeing.

There is a concept termed "bardo" in Dzogchen literature which is often a way of recognizing the Alaya of habits. "Bardo" usually refers to the space and time continuum between death and crystallizing into the next birth. It is also defined as the space and time continuum between two conceptual cognitive elements where the Alaya of habits and rigpa can be recognized. But before that, you must learn and train yourself in meditation techniques to recognize the cognitive spaces between two words, thoughts, and feelings.

The Method of Meditation

You mustn't be distracted by sensory cognition during your meditation session. Therefore, Dzogchen meditation is recommended to be done in total silence and total darkness using three immovables, namely:

Immovable Body - Your body should be straight. Your hands should be in a meditation pose or resting lightly on your knees.

Immovable Senses - Darkness and silence would take care of all your other senses. Your eyes should be neither fully closed nor fully open. Gently gaze naturally in front of you.

Immovable Mind - Immovable mind is about letting go of "active thinking." It deals with letting go of thoughts from the past and the visions of the future. It also means not analyzing thoughts and allowing them to freely come and leave your mind. Even if thoughts arise (which they will, especially with beginners), you must not follow or engage with them. By doing so, you are allowing thoughts to dissolve into nothingness.

With these three immovables, meditation allows you to just remain and rest in the present moment of awareness. This moment is not contaminated with thoughts from the past or future and is fresh and contrived. This moment is free of self-consciousness about our behavior and our actions.

Verbal thoughts will simultaneously arise, reach a peak, and cease automatically when we don't engage or follow them. On repeating this process, you will slowly but surely find the "gaps" between two thoughts where the Alaya of habits can be recognized.

An important element in this meditation technique is not to "simply stop" your thoughts by applying discipline or restraint. Controlling your thoughts is not the plan of Dzogchen meditation. Thoughts will arise, peak, and cease automatically on their own and require no effort from your side. You cannot really stop thoughts coming into your mind, at least not as a beginner.

The trick is to be conscious of thoughts and the path they take in your mind. Your effort should be focused on recognizing the thoughts as they pass your mind. Your effort should be focused on consciously understanding and being aware of your thoughts without reacting or responding to them. Without this conscious effort to understand your thoughts, there will either be mental wandering (where you simply follow your thoughts mindlessly) or mental dullness (where you fall into a daze as the avalanche of thoughts hits you).

Madhyamaka Analytical Meditation

Dzogchen meditation is not about analyzing our verbal thoughts. Analysis does not result in understanding or realization. But, to focus on understanding the arising, abiding, and cessation of verbal thoughts, a student must necessarily learn about voidness or emptiness through an analytical method called "searching for the hidden flaw of the mind." This analysis consists of these elements:

- Where does the thought or verbal thinking originate?
- How does the thought reside or remain in the moment?
- When and where does it disappear or ceases?

Searching for the hidden flaw in the mind is what Madhyamaka analysis is all about. It goes about analyzing everything, including events and thoughts right from their origin (or cause), the event or thought itself, and its effects. Only when you can discern between the moments of verbal thinking can you understand the simultaneity of the three elements of an event or thought.

Slowly your meditation progresses into subtler levels than just verbal thoughts. You begin to meditate on these elements as well:
- Thoughts or verbal thinking
- Mental images
- Feelings of sadness, happiness, jealousy, and neutral feelings too
- Attitudes such as expectation, disappointment, hope, boredom
- The conceptual construction of blankness we experience as "this" or "that"

Another important thing to learn and master before Dzogchen meditation is understanding the complete absence of a separate, monolithic, and unaffected "you" or "me" as the initiator and controller of verbal thinking. You must understand these thoughts happen automatically with no effort from anyone. There is no "me" creating the thoughts.

We might still be far away from recognizing the Alaya of habits with all the meditation mentioned above. For further help, the Dzogchen masters are always available.

When you have perfected your meditation and can identify the Alaya of habits, it's time now to know and realize rigpa face-to-face. Before that, let us understand a little more about rigpa and its opposite, Marigpa.

Marigpa - The Opposite of Rigpa

Marigpa - The opposite of rigpa is marigpa. It means "avidya" in Sanskrit, which means "ignorance." Literally translating to "without illumination," marigpa is the Tibetan term that describes the illusion sentient beings suffer from when they are disconnected from the true nature of reality.

Importantly, marigpa does not translate to being stupid or foolish. You could be intelligent, clever, and even possess wisdom. However, you cannot realize the wisdom you possess. You don't see things clearly and don't understand the true nature of reality.

According to Tibetan Buddhism, ignorance is the root cause of all suffering and the primary reason we all come into the space of afflictions. The space of afflictions is rife with sentient beings clinging on and attaching themselves to all phenomena because they are under the impact of Marigpa. They are ignorant of the true nature of reality.

Marigpa can, therefore, be described as the state in which sentient beings cannot understand the full meaning and deep implications of the four noble truths. In Tibetan Buddhism, Marigpa is defined as:

The first link in the 12 links of dependent origination. Dependent origination is an important Buddhist concept that states that all inner and outer phenomena depend on different causes. No phenomenon appears without a cause. The twelve links are a set of 12 Buddhist teachings that progress in stages, beginning from acknowledging Marigpa and ending with old age and death, describing the cycle of samsara.

The twelve links are as follows (interestingly, each link has an image connected with it):

Ignorance - Marigpa of the fundamental ignorance regarding the true nature of reality and the delusion of believing that the five aggregates together form the "self." The image of the first link is that of a blind man groping his way around using a cane.

Formation - Also called karma formation, this second link follows from ignorance. As long as there is marigpa, karma is continuously created and recreated, resulting in rebirths in different realms. The image connected with formation is that of a potter creating a pot on his wheel.

Consciousness - Formations result in the consciousness of the next existence once all the conditions of causes and effects come together. This is represented by a monkey swinging from one tree to another. An image that is similar to the way our mind swings from one thought to another.

Name and form - Through the power of consciousness of the next existence along with the five aggregates (Sanskrit: skandhas), we get linked to a womb where our body develops a name and form. A person (or a group of people) in a boat is the image used to represent this link. The five aggregates or skandhas that give rise to the concept of "self" require:

- A physical body
- A form (which is the boat)
- A psyche
- A name (consisting of the four mental skandhas including feeling, perception, mental formations, and consciousness)

The six ayatanas - With the formation of name and form, the six ayatanas (or sense organs) connected with the sense faculties emerge. The six sense organs are represented by an image of five windows and a door because these organs are the gateway through which the outer world is perceived and experienced.

Contact - This stage is the coming together of the sense faculties, objects, and consciousness. The image of this link is a couple in an embrace.

Sensation - Sensation arises from contact. Sensations include the neutral, pleasant, and unpleasant. The image associated with this link is a person with an arrow in his eye.

Craving - From sensations arise the craving to not be separated from pleasurable sensations and be separated from unpleasant sensations. This is represented by the image of a lady offering a drink to a man.

Grasping - Increased craving leads to grasping, which is a state of the active struggle of attracting pleasurable cravings and avoiding unpleasant, painful ones. The image linked to grasping is that of a man plucking fruit from a tree.

Becoming - Through this grasp, the cycle of karma formation begins again, determining the next existence. "Becoming" is represented by multiple images, including a pregnant woman, a couple making love, and a beautiful bride.

Rebirth - Through the power of becoming, there is rebirth. This happens according to accumulated karma and when the conditions have all been assembled. The image of rebirth is that of a woman giving birth.

Old age and death - Old age and death follow rebirth. The process of aging happens as the five aggregates change and develop. Death happens when the five aggregates cease. Old age and death are represented by the image of a corpse born by four pall-bearers.

Dzogchen is rooted in Vajrayana. Vajrayana is similar to a thunderbolt that destroys all ignorance and obscurations that prevent you from knowing and realizing rigpa, the wisdom of pure awareness.

There are basically two methods through which you can know rigpa face-to-face. One method simply relies on the outer inspiration from Dzogchen masters and the inner circumstance of basic rigpa or pure awareness or Buddha-nature inherent in all sentient beings.

You can also rely on six key points to know rigpa face-to-face, and these six points that fit into a student's meditation practice include:
- Holding the attention of your mind
- Keeping your mind stable or at rest
- Understanding the root of the matter
- Eliminating the sense of substantiality normally associated with all phenomena. When this sense of substantiality is gotten rid of, the mind does not follow an object or thought or event because it knows that there is nowhere to go.
- Using the interval between objects and awareness of these objects
- Causing sudden distraction - for example, loudly shouting "phat"

The last method mentioned is common and quite popular among students of Dzogchen practice. When we are startled or distracted suddenly, for an instant, our thoughts come to a standstill.

Most people, at this stage, cannot recognize rigpa. They can only connect with the Alaya of habits or the intervening space between two moments of thoughts or events. Alaya of habits is limited awareness and can be defined only as a bedazzled or dumbfounded factor of not knowing rigpa. Yet, recognizing the Alaya of habits is one step forward in awakening your rigpa.

The Effulgent Rigpa

You mustn't confuse Alaya of habits with the realization of rigpa. It is equally important not to confuse the realization of decisive awareness (producing and perceiving cognitive appearances) or the deepest nature (consists of emptiness or voidness) with the Alaya of habits.

Dzogchen practice goes deeper than the Alaya of habits and recognizing conventional awareness. It is subtler and deeper than mere recognition of moments of verbal thinking. Dzogchen practice recognizes a cognitive space between two moments or thoughts with a deep awareness of its own.

When we find this cognitive space, then dumbfoundedness ceases, and the Alaya of habits becomes rigpa. This is possible only by greasing our minds with previous preparatory meditation practices involving clearing the pathways of our energy channels using mantras and tantras.

When we do this, we recognize the effulgent rigpa, an aspect of rigpa that gives rise to cognitive appearances along with actively recognizing them. In effulgent rigpa, the activity of giving rise to cognitive appearances is more prominent than actively recognizing them. With repeated practice using Buddha figures, effulgent rigpa recognizes itself as the rainbow body instead of the ordinary five gross aggregates.

The Essence Rigpa

After recognizing and being able to stay focused with effulgent rigpa, you can recognize essence rigpa. This aspect of rigpa consists of open space (or klong), also called cognitive sphere (or dbyings). Here too, there is an arising of cognitive appearances and cognizing them. However, in essence, rigpa, cognizing appearances is more prominent than giving rise to cognitive appearances.

When you practice and perfect meditation to where you can recognize and stay focused on the essence rigpa, then you attain a remarkable breakthrough. This is called "thregs-chod," or "seeing the pathway of the mind."

At the leap-ahead stage, or "thod-rgal," effulgent rigpa becomes increasingly prominent even while the essence rigpa simultaneously becomes prominent.

Accessing rigpa is equivalent to achieving the primordial state of mindfulness, which is why Dzogchen is often called non-meditation or effortless meditation or non-deliberate meditation.

Chapter 10: The Semdzin Practice

The Semdzin practice is designed to help us see the true nature of reality. They are short practices consisting of different kinds of visualizations and mantras. When you use them and practice Semdzin meditations regularly, you can access the natural state of your being.

"Sem" translates to "nature of the mind," and "dzin" translates to "hold." Therefore, Semdzin means "to hold the nature of the mind." In other words, it means to "recognize the true nature of the mind" using simple techniques.

Some semdzin practices include:
- The Semdzin on the Aa sound
- The Semdzin on the syllable "phat"
- The Semdzin on the joyous laughter of the wrathful manifestations
- The Semdzin on the struggle of the Asuras
- The Semdzin on the letter RAM
- The Semdzin on the HUM that chases thoughts
- The Semdzin on the Song of the Vajra.

Let us look at some of these seven practices in a bit of detail.

The Semdzin on the syllable "phat" - The syllable "phat" helps cut a hole and clear the entanglement between the subject and object. The sound of "phat" is practiced in a way that it comes from deep inside us. It rises to the top of our head in full strength so there is a cut in our verbal thoughts, which creates the duality cocoon around us. This cocoon prevents us from seeing the true non-dual nature of reality.

The loud and clear uttering of the syllable "phat" should serve the purpose of converting our seemingly familiar and friendly verbal thoughts into our enemy. Here is an analogy to explain this concept.

Before the world realized the hugely harmful effects of smoking, can you recall how the habit of smoking was perceived? Most people who started the smoking habit thought it made them look cool and sophisticated. That is how the association with smoking was built up in those days. Now, anti-smoking campaigns are on the rise, designed to re-frame the perception of smoking from cool and sophisticated to extremely dangerous for health.

The Semdzin practice of the syllable "phat" works similarly. We have been led to believe that our thoughts are "good" because they give us a sense of identity by rendering a "known" space of experience. Our thoughts create an intoxicating cocoon filled with feelings and unconscious, mindless actions and activities that take us deeper into the cycle of suffering-filled suffering. The function of our thoughts works against learning the true identity of nature. Our thoughts come in the way of getting a clear, non-muddy mind, a key element to getting extraordinary insight.

Remember that rigpa or pure awareness is, as its name suggests, "pure, naked, and unchanging." It is already there in all of us and can never be removed. Only the covering of the cocoon that is preventing us from seeing rigpa face-to-face needs to be removed. The Semdzin practice of the syllable "phat" is a great tool towards this goal. Getting wrapped up in our family, cozy thoughts give us false reassurances that these thoughts are "me." These thoughts compel us to accept the wrong idea that "This is me." The "phat" syllable helps us to break this bad habit.

The "phat" syllable is effectively cutting through the idea that "I am an object." When we have the idea of us being an object, then others' opinions rule our lives. We are tormented by questions such as:
- What will people think of me?
- What if people don't like what I am doing?

Instead of analyzing these questions (which you will realize are worthless when you achieve realization), you can cut through these conceptions using the "phat" syllable.

The Semdzin practice of "phat" is quite easy. Sit in a comfortable, easy position and meditate. Every time you are disturbed by a sound or thought that threatens to take away the power of your meditation, say loudly, "phat." This sound cuts a hole and disconnects the bind linking the subject and object, namely yourself and the thought and/or sense perception.

An easy and gentle way of using the "phat" semdzin practice is to take a short break from your routine. Go to the countryside or any unfamiliar place, and keep repeating "phat" for an entire day. This exercise can free your body and mind of burdens that were lurking around and holding you down.

After this short exercise, you will feel light and get the urge to stand up and dance and laugh and move around freely. Considering that this outcome might make you look "strange" to others watching, it might be wise to try it in an isolated, undisturbed place. This kind of place is also ideal because it allows you to have an unimpeded connection between the infinity of the world and the infinity of your heart.

Laughter, which would be an outcome of the "phat" exercise, makes you happy and loosens your diaphragm. Further, laughing and dancing help you remove hitherto invisible or difficult-to-remove barriers of self-consciousness that are required to be cut through. This exercise helps with that too. It is considered to be a practice of fearlessness.

A more elaborate and difficult practice is described in Machig Labdron chod (the Tibetan term for spiritual practice). Machig Labdron, which translates to "Singular Mother Torch from Lab," was a renowned Tibetan Buddhist tantric master who lived in the 10th-11th century. Many Vajrayana lineages originated from this revered yogini.

According to the chod described by her, one of the first things you must do is leave your own body to become a daikini (a wise being freed from your body). Then, you cut up your body into pieces and make a kind of a stew inside your skull. Then you invite all beings right from the highest buddha to the local demons to partake of the stew you have prepared using your own body. The feast goes on until there is nothing left of your stewed body.

Now, there is no body, and there is nothing to go back to. When you have finished your meditation, you have a form, of course. However, this form is not the same as the one you sat down for meditation. That body has been cooked and eaten.

This elaborate form of meditation is an effective tool to empty your body of all preconceived assumptions. According to Buddhism, our body and its attached senses is not a problem. The problem arises when we fill it with associations, thoughts, and habits that hold us captive and prevent our freedom.

This meditation practice also helps you become increasingly aware of your body and its various associations. When you are aware of your body, the syllable "phat" can be repeatedly employed until you eliminate all senses of contact with your body. At this stage, you become open space. This exercise needs to be repeated and practiced many times over before you can achieve sustained success.

A word of caution at this stage is vital. This technique should not be used if you grapple with mind-related issues such as psychotic episodes, depersonalization, etc. It is a disruption technique that will likely worsen your mental condition because it drives you away from familiarity, which is vital for stability in the materialistic world. Therefore, if you have a mental issue, do not try this technique without approval from your doctor.

The Aa Practice - The Aa practice is a simply releasing process using the sound of "Aa." This practice also proves there is no difference between our inner and outer worlds. Because if there was a difference, then the "Aa" practice would not have worked. It works because there is no duality and differences.

The Aa practice works because, in reality, there is no illusion of duality created and maintained by our mental activity. The recitation of Aa is not an effort to make anything happen. It is just an exercise to release and undo the active forces of obscuration that prevent you from knowing and identifying the Alaya of habits, and eventually, rigpa.

So, how does our mental activity create an illusion of duality or separation? Here is an analogy to explain it. Suppose you light the end of a stick, and it starts to burn. Now, there is only one fire. Next, start twirling the stick around in circles. You will see a circle of fire. This circle, as you know, is an illusion. There is, in reality, only one source of fire at the end of the stick. The same thing happens in our life experiences based largely on our emotions and mental activity. Our mental activity is so rapid that we perceive diversity in the world. Consequently, we are blinded from seeing the true, non-dualistic nature of reality.

Here is another example of how illusion drives afflictive emotions in our lives. Suppose you are walking on a dark path. Suddenly you see a snake lying just ahead of you. Your mind is filled with fear. Then, you realize that it is not a snake but just a harmless piece of rope. You are extremely relieved. When the illusion of seeing it as a snake vanishes, the true reality of that element is visible to you. When you practice Dzogchen meditation, the illusion of duality vanishes, and you get to see the true, unfiltered, and pure nature of reality.

The struggle against suffering is nothing more than the struggle with our afflictive emotions. One thought and/or one afflictive emotion struggles with another. And this struggle is relentless without a single moment of pause. Here is an interesting analogy to explain this struggle.

Suppose two brothers are lying side by side on the bed. One brother is awake while the other brother is asleep, experiencing a nightmare. The brother who is awake is trying to wake up the sleeping brother. Once the sleeping brother wakes up, he is not in any danger. However, even when he was in the dream, he was not really in any danger. And this is the core aspect of emptiness. Everything is an illusion, and nothing actually exists.

Everything that worries us makes us anxious and burdensome, and even those elements that make us seem happy are all a construct of our mind. There is no need to try very hard to get rid of burdens because they are not real. Our effort to get rid of it, in fact, enhances the burden and anxiety.

Rigpa or pure, naked awareness is already inherent and part of all of us. We need only to relax the mind. Unceasing thoughts and mental activity will arise to create new patterns that smudge the pathway to rigpa. We only need to allow these firefly-like thoughts and ideas to settle down harmlessly like mud in an undisturbed lake. This will allow the pathway to be clear without obscurations. Dzogchen practice does exactly this.

The Aa practice is very easy to do. You need only to sit in a quiet, undisturbed place and release the Aa sound. Then, sit in the present moment and open yourself to accept everything that comes to you. In this state, many things and appearances will come to you. And you will have your own interpretations as well.

You can label what is coming to you as right or wrong, good or bad, or form any judgment. You simply must remember these judgments and formations are merely your mind's construct. Since you are not grounded in emptiness, your mind gets into conclusions and judgments, and samsara keeps rolling on.

Everything that happens is the combination of whatever arises with your reactions and/or responses. Whatever may happen, every moment is available for you to see and experience in its entirety. The primary goal of meditation is to see for ourselves how we create storylines, narratives, and consequently, our reactions and responses to our thoughts, hoping to see clarity. However, as we meditate and get more practice, we realize these mental activities are not clarifying anything. Instead, they are muddying the already, deeply muddied waters of our minds.

The more you see the storylines created by your mind, the more you will realize it is part of a million storylines created by every other sentient being in the world. These stories mingle with each other and create more stories, often changing our own narratives and thoughts.

When we realize the confusion caused by our minds through meditation, we automatically build compassion. This is because we identify and accept there is nothing we can do to control our thoughts. Remember, our thoughts do not capture us. We are holding on to our thoughts. When we let go of them, we realize freedom. The more we let go of them, the more we get closer to the Alaya of habits and rigpa and further away from marigpa.

Chapter 11: The Trekcho Practice

Buddhism says that all phenomena are nothing but the manifestations and perceptions of your mind. Everything you see and sense within and around you are contained in one. Even the levels of attained rigpa, namely the ground, path, and fruition, are all constructs of our mind. In reality, there are no levels because there is no duality.

To give you an analogy, if you have a toffee wrapped in paper, then the paper is the ground, the wrapper is the path, and the opening of the wrapper is the fruition. The sweet toffee has always been inside the wrapper. You can access that sweetness only after going through the activity of unwrapping it.

The essence of nature is beyond permanence and impermanence. Actually, it is outside all phenomena. However, we are caught up in the phenomena of "this" and "that" and don't recognize the natural state of being. In fact, all phenomena we experience and sense are already awakened. We believe in the phenomena because that is what we experience. But, in the true reality, nothing exists, and no phenomenon has any existence.

Sentient beings who have not achieved enlightenment cannot remain in the natural state of rest and voidness at all points in time. Therefore, it is easy to fall into the trap of believing that our delusions and illusions are all true. Many beings are in the natural state of rest at all times. And they can see the true nature of reality.

But for us, as long as we are in the deluded state and have not been able to achieve rigpa, we remain in a state of illusion and believe it to be the true, natural state. The Trekcho practice helps us break down the walls and shells of delusion to see the true nature of reality. When the shells fall apart, we let go of grasping and clinging to illusionary phenomena, and the natural state will automatically reveal itself.

Understanding Kadag Trekcho

The Menngagde teachings are divided into indivisible aspects, namely:
- Kadag Trekcho
- Lhubdrub Togal

This chapter is dedicated to Trekcho, while the next one is for Togal. Trekcho is "cutting through the things we need to give up." Before going into details of Trekcho practice, let us summarize the three important points given by Garab Dorje.
- Recognize the nature of your mind.
- Recognize rigpa but also leave a lot of space around it.
- Be confident that you can and will achieve liberation. Don't doubt it. Just feel your confidence about achieving liberation.

Trekcho is the thorough cutting through the obscurations to pieces. Trekcho means to slash through the obscurations as you would with a knife. The previous thought has ended, and the next one is yet to arise. The knife of Trekcho is used to slash through the "stream of present moments."

As you keep slashing through the various present moments you encounter, the "string of your relentless thoughts" will fall into pieces and disappear or be liberated. The "string of thoughts or the "stream of present moments" are the backbone of obscurations, and when these are slashed, the pathway to pure awareness becomes increasingly clear.

Letting go of emotions alone is not enough to become liberated. To achieve liberation, we have to let go of our sense of "self," which prevents us from knowing rigpa. When we recognize the emptiness of our mind, then we can let go of our clinging ego. When we achieve natural clarity, all qualities unfold automatically.

Natural clarity is also part of samsara, and it can see and connect with your ego lurking behind. When this clarity sees and identifies the natural openness, then it merges with emptiness. Freeing yourself from emotions and obscurations gives rise to faith.

When you identify with the emptiness of your emotions, you learn to look at your life from a new, refreshing perspective. You can let go of binding and clinging emotions and bring happiness and joy to your life. You realize your emotions are not real. You lose fear too. This state of letting go of emotions can be compared to the birth of a new baby, ready to grow and develop into a faithful and clear-headed adult.

However, it is also important to know that "faith" in the Buddhist context is not about clinging to religious ideology. It is about knowing and accepting that rigpa or "pure awareness" is inherent in all of us, and every one of us can achieve enlightenment. The clinging kind of faith is dangerous too because it causes attachment and enhances obscurations.

When you achieve enlightenment, the body and the subtle energy channels become Vajra-body. Your mind becomes Vajra-mind, and your speech becomes Vajra-speech. You can have strong clarity, and everything you see is crystal clear to you. However, if the clarity is very strong, then you may get stuck in it. If that happens, freeing yourself from this position becomes difficult.

Therefore, it is important to have open space when you recognize rigpa. Another element you will experience is bliss which is a good thing. However, with bliss comes attachment, and getting rid of this attachment is difficult too. Therefore, you must be ready to give up what you gained to achieve the highest level of Dzogchen wisdom.

Meditation to Achieve Trekcho

- Knowing the actual nature of the mind requires meditation on these points:
- Continuously reflect on the impermanence that surrounds us.
- Focus on the trials and tribulations of samsara.
- Change your behavior to align with the laws of cause and effect.
- Maintain a stable state of resting mind and an altruistic intention. With this foundation, ensure all your actions of body, mind, and speech are beneficial to others.
- Accumulate merit and create prayers of aspirations. Conscientiously, work on accumulating merit and purifying yourself.

Meditate on these elements to realize the unborn, inherent awareness within you. You must practice these until you have achieved uncontrived devotion to your master and continue to keep your devotion until you reach enlightenment. Here is a great prayer to use to fall back on the blessings and spiritual power of your master or the guru of your chosen lineage:

- The outer lineage prayer - to visualize your master and his blessings all around you.
- The inner prayer - to know and realize that your inner and outer master are the same.
- The secret prayer - to connect with and stay with the secret inner master, namely rigpa.

When you connect with your inner lineage master, you connect with rigpa, and in this state, you are connected with all the Buddhas in the higher realms. It is like having a hotline with all the Buddhas.

In your journey towards finding the true nature of reality, you will learn that your mind is the most important factor and contributor to making us wander aimlessly through repeated births and rebirths in samsara. Next, we look for hidden flaws in the mind. As we progress in this journey, we focus on examining the body, mind, and speech factors to see whether they are one of three separate entities.

This journey of searching for hidden flaws will continue until you realize that although at a conventional level, the three appear distinct, in reality, there is nothing distinct. There is no real entity called the "mind," which is distinct by itself. Even the concept of our mind is an illusion, a mere appearance of something unreal and non-existent.

In the same way all external phenomena have no real existence but are mere illusions, you will realize your mind also lacks a presence. There is no real existence or presence of the mind and has no origin or foundation. The mind searching and the mind that is being sought are one and the same and are unreal. One merely gives rise to the other. Clinging on to our fleeting thoughts caused by fleeting conditions and causes, we all go through the delusion of samsara rife with suffering.

As you practice trekcho meditation using the three doors of body, mind, and speech, you will experience intermittent states of non-conceptual clarity. These fluctuating visions of non-conceptual clarity could be in the form of bliss or a clear, thought-free mind. Even these mental experiences are flawed.

Regardless of our mental experiences, which could be in the form of obscurations, the important thing to do is maintain awareness of the present. The present moment cannot be transformed, harmed, or benefitted from any of our mental activities or experiences.

The awareness of the present moment is unsullied, fresh, unspoiled, and uncontrived. It is lucid, nakedly apparent, and beyond any concrete verbal definition. The only way to know it is to experience it. This clear, unsullied, and penetrating awareness is not a void, nor is it empty. It is the primordial awareness whose essence is undefinable and has existed since the dawn of the cosmos. This is rigpa, and how to sustain this awareness is to use these four ways of leaving things:

- Leave the view as it is, like a mountain
- Leave the meditation as it is, like the ocean
- Leave the appearances and actions as they are
- Leave the fruition (rigpa) as it is

This phenomenon of four ways of leaving things is the method used to introduce the rigpa directly face-to-face, in, and as itself. And for this, we must have confidence in the concept that there is no other "buddha" but the one within all sentient beings, inherently. This primordial state of being is the only "buddha." Everyone who has reached this state and sustained it eternally becomes buddhas.

Meditation calls for and means not to waver from the point of view or experience without being distracted, fixated, or clinging to it. During meditation, you must not try to block out the experiences of your senses. You should also not allow your attention to stray or be distracted, scattered, or withdrawn.

Meditation is about allowing everything in your mind to come forth and settle naturally with no effort from your side. The only thing you must do while meditating is not to show restraint to anything. As there is no duality between experiences and the experiencer, objects and subjects, etc., simply allowing everything to disappear on its own.

In this context, "disappearing" means to "dissolve into nothingness," just like the path of a flying bird. You must have confidence that all rising thoughts will dissolve into nothing. Exercising no restraint or control, if you practice meditation like this, you will realize the truth that things simply die on their own with no effort from your side. Remaining unmoving is a key aspect of meditation, both during meditation as well as post-meditation.

While meditating, your thoughts will go all over the place even though you are sitting in one place. The trick is in sitting through it without doing anything. If you experience rigpa and get thrown out of that state instantaneously, don't fight your way back in. This effort is not only useless but also counterproductive to meditation. You will lose the view again.

A bigger mistake you can make to yourself is believe that your meditation is "not good." Your meditative experiences will be jeopardized. You simply have to sit through the ups and downs of your thoughts. You have to cut through your laziness and sit for your meditation sessions daily and consistently.

An analogy of a snow-lion is used to explain meditation-related frustrations, especially when nothing "worthy is happening." A snow lion does not attack the stones when the stones are thrown. It waits patiently and attacks the stone-thrower. In the same way, attack the root of your suffering, not the manifestations of your sufferings that come in the form of mindless thoughts and afflictive emotions.

While staying in a relaxed meditative state, look at your mind grasping and clinging to everything thrown at it. If you persevere, even if you cannot achieve the non-dual rigpa status and continue to experience non-dualistic clinging, these experiences will not become obscurations. They will be like clouds in the sky that are there but do not sully the purity of the sky.

Your dualistic experiences will not taint your ability to see the true nature of reality, and the two kinds of obscurations will disappear along with your habitual tendencies. Consequently, your experience with the primordial state of wisdom, or rigpa, will increase. A piece of final advice to beginners is to remain unattached to any and all meditative experiences. This includes moods and visions, both positive and negative. You should not suppress or aggravate any experience. Instead, you must simply allow them to unfold on their own.

To summarize, Trekcho practice helps you develop a state of mind that cuts through basic spiritual materialism. When this is done, there is nothing left to cut anymore. As you progress in this practice, you will realize cutting through and eliminating spiritual materialism itself can be a form of spiritual materialism if you get attached to it. And finally, you will realize that cutting through also becomes a questionable activity. So, the next step would be to move to Togal practice.

Chapter 12: The Togal Path

Togal translates to "direct crossing," and, along with Trekcho, is one of two important aspects of Dzogchen practice. Togal also means "leapover" or "the direct approach." The Togal path can quickly bring about the realization of the three kayas in this lifetime itself. The Togal path has the power to reveal all aspects of enlightenment within this lifetime of the practitioner. Therefore, it is a faster way of dissolving your karmic vision.

To reach the Togal Path requires you to complete these steps:

First, know and understand what Dzogchen or the Great Perfection is all about. It is the direct realization of what is mentioned in the "Heart Sutra" about seeing all phenomena without the muddying effects of obscurations. Dzogchen teaching uses the analogy of a clear, unmuddied lake to explain how to see all phenomena.

- The water is clear and clean right down to the lake bed.
- Fishes and other aquatic animals are swimming around as they should.
- The sky above is wide and clear.
- And the birds are flying as birds should.
-

This verse shows that it is essential for Dzogchen practitioners to first see everything and accept it as it is. There is no need to change or alter anything because all phenomena we experience with our five senses are as they should be.

The next step in the Dzogchen path is to see the true nature of reality. It requires you to let go of clinging and attachment to your ego and the phenomena that you experience to do so. The third step, which consists of Trekcho and Togal, is about two different aspects of cultivating the true nature you have identified and experienced continually.

The practice of Togal brings about the realization of the spontaneous presence. This is the nature of the ground of Dzogchen into and from which all phenomena dissolve and arise. The practice of Togal should be done by a practitioner who has gained sufficiently high levels of competence in the Trekcho practice. Togal practice is designed to cultivate clear light visions that are over and above the natural state of mind.

Moreover, the Togal path should be introduced by your Dzogchen master. When he or she feels you have a thorough grounding in Trekcho, only then will your master introduce you to the advanced practice of Togal. A Togal practitioner uses extremely powerful exercises to work directly with the clear light, or the spontaneous presence, to reveal this light within himself or herself.

Togal can be instantaneous, which means you can achieve enlightenment in an instant. An analogy would be a traveler who physically travels over steep hills and valleys to reach the mountain peak. With Togal, the practitioner can "leap over" to the desired peak (realization of rigpa) instantly.

For this reason, the Togal path is considered a unique and extraordinary Dzogchen practice. Trekcho is the wisdom of Dzogchen, and Togal is the skillful means. Togal practice calls for enormous discipline and restraint and is almost always practiced in a retreat environment away from the hustle-bustle of daily life.

Therefore the Togal practice should be followed only under the strict supervision and guidance of a qualified, senior, and experienced Dzogchen master.

The Togal Path for a Beginner

As a beginner, you can experience the Togal path by following certain Togal instructions. In these instructed exercises, you are supposed to listen to sounds emanating from your inner sound visions. It is believed that Avalokiteshwara used this method to achieve enlightenment.

The sound is supposed to be a very silent one which becomes loud as you advance in the Togal path. However, for this exercise to succeed, practitioners must receive the instructions from a master, without which the practice road is difficult and likely to fail.

The realization achieved through Togal results in knowing and realizing the vastness of space with no sense of boundary, making all phenomena the same. There is a total absence of duality. The space you experience has no fear or hope, pleasure or pain, or any afflictive emotions and phenomena, and nothing to hold on to.

You just experience and understand that space is nothing and has no value at all. The Togal path can begin only after studying and perfecting shamatha and vipassana as well as completing trekcho. The thing about Togal is that there is no point in coming to this stage until and unless you have realized effulgent rigpa and essence rigpa. Even the kindest and open-minded masters may not agree to take you through the Togal practice until then.

A Simple, Powerful Prayer to Dzogchen Masters

I salute and pray to Dharmakaya Samantabhadra and his consort.

I pray to the lord of the great Vajradhara, the sixth Buddha family.

I pray to the teacher Vajrasattva.

I pray to the Vidyadhara Garab Dorje.

I pray to Guru Sri Simha.

I pray to the eight Vidyadharas of India.

I pray to Padmakara, the one who is deathless.

I pray to Princess Mandharava, and to the kings and subjects, and the 25 disciples, and to the 108 revealers of treasure.

I pray to the lineage gurus and to the gracious root.

I pray to the 42 peaceful deities. I pray to pure vidyadhara and consort.

I pray to the 50 blazing herukas.

I pray to the five classes of daikinis who keep and maintain the dharma.

I pray to all the people who have taken an oath to be protectors of the dharma

I pray and seek the blessings and guidance of my lama, guru, master.

In the presence of my guru, I eliminate all self-based confusions and conflicts.

I pray that I may directly see the dharmata through your blessings.

I seek your blessings and inspirations so that my visionary experiences grow and develop.

I seek your blessings so that I may achieve pure awareness of its full potential.

I seek your blessings so that I may reach the level of exhaustion in dharmata.

I seek your blessings so that I may achieve the rainbow body.

I seek your blessings so that I may practice and perfect the great transference.

I seek your blessings so that I may achieve Buddhahood in this lifetime.

Conclusion

We must not waste the privilege to be born as humans. Suffering-filled samsara, the eternal cycle of potential births and rebirths, has a small door for escape. That door comes in the form of being as a human. Human birth is even more precious if we have access to something that will free us from the clutches of samsaric suffering.

The most important lesson you can get from Dzogchen practice is that most our problems are rooted in our minds. If we can find the strength to manage our minds, most our problems will disappear.

Of course, there are other forms of consciousness around you. Another person processes the world around them differently than you do, and there is nothing you can do to control that. So, if a jealous or angry individual treats you in an unpleasant way, you cannot really stop them from doing that. However, the way you react or respond to the person is something you manage because that stems from your mind.

Dzogchen is that wonderful tool that has this potential. Therefore, it makes sense to start your journey and practice what is in this book diligently and committedly. The most important thing about Buddhism is compassion for all, including yourself, called self-compassion. Be kind and compassionate with yourself as you learn the difficult but extremely useful ropes of Dzogchen and find the doorway to freedom and unbounded joy and happiness.

Now, go back, reread the book slowly this time, understand the concepts within, and practice the recommendations and suggestions at home patiently and diligently. There is wondrous light waiting for you at the end of the journey.

Here's another book by Mari Silva that you might like

Your Free Gift (only available for a limited time)

Thanks for getting this book! If you want to learn more about various spirituality topics, then join Mari Silva's community and get a free guided meditation MP3 for awakening your third eye. This guided meditation mp3 is designed to open and strengthen ones third eye so you can experience a higher state of consciousness. Simply visit the link below the image to get started.

https://spiritualityspot.com/meditation

References

A Brief Presentation of the Nine Vehicles. (n.d.). Www.lotsawahouse.org. Retrieved from https://www.lotsawahouse.org/tibetan-masters/alak-zenkar/nine-yanas

A Glimpse of Dzogchen. (2017, March 6). Shambhala. https://www.shambhala.com/snowlion_articles/a-glimpse-of-dzogchen-by-sogyal-rinpoche/

Aro - An uncommon perspective. (n.d.). Arobuddhism.org. Retrieved from https://arobuddhism.org/community/an-uncommon-perspective.html

Commentary on the Seven Points of Mind Training. (n.d.). Www.lotsawahouse.org. Retrieved from https://www.lotsawahouse.org/tibetan-masters/gyalse-thogme-zangpo/commentary-on-seven-points-mind-training

Complete Dzogchen Teaching on Karma Lingpa's "Beholding Naked Awareness." (n.d.). Www.youtube.com. Retrieved from https://youtu.be/aA-YU2cW5_g

Dzogchen. (n.d.). Www.sacred-Texts.com. Retrieved from https://www.sacred-texts.com/bud/tib/dzgchnsd.htm

Dzogchen and the Nine Vehicles of Enlightenment – David Paul Boaz. (n.d.). Retrieved from https://davidpaulboaz.org/religious-studies/dzogchen-and-the-nine-vehicles-of-enlightenment/

Dzogchen Series. (n.d.). Www.lotsawahouse.org. Retrieved from https://www.lotsawahouse.org/topics/dzogchen/

Dzogchen Teaching. (n.d.). Www.youtube.com. Retrieved from https://youtu.be/o23bYf59ZtE

Key Points on Trekchö. (n.d.). Www.lotsawahouse.org. Retrieved from https://www.lotsawahouse.org/tibetan-masters/jamyang-khyentse-chokyi-lodro/key-points-on-trekcho

Menngagde - Chinese Buddhist Encyclopedia. (n.d.). Chinabuddhismencyclopedia.com. Retrieved from http://tibetanbuddhistencyclopedia.com/en/index.php/Menngagde

Nine yanas - Rigpa Wiki. (n.d.). Www.rigpawiki.org. Retrieved from https://www.rigpawiki.org/index.php?title=Nine_yanas

PBS. (2019). Basics of Buddhism. Pbs.org. https://www.pbs.org/edens/thailand/buddhism.htm

Semde | Project Gutenberg Self-Publishing - eBooks | Read eBooks online. (n.d.). Www.self.gutenberg.org. Retrieved from http://www.self.gutenberg.org/articles/eng/Semde

Seven Points of Mind Training. (n.d.). Www.lotsawahouse.org. Retrieved from https://www.lotsawahouse.org/tibetan-masters/geshe-chekhawa-yeshe-dorje/seven-points-mind-training

The Nine Vehicles According to Nyingma. (n.d.). Studybuddhism.com. https://studybuddhism.com/en/advanced-studies/vajrayana/dzogchen-advanced/the-nine-vehicles-according-to-nyingma

Vajragoni. (n.d.). The Cuckoo of Presence | UnbornMind Zen. Retrieved from https://unbornmind.com/2019/01/29/the-cuckoo-of-presence/

Lightning Source UK Ltd.
Milton Keynes UK
UKHW020041121021
392037UK00008B/1578